Key Rates and Data: Employment 2018/2019

Written and compiled by
Croner-i

Revised and updated by

Sarah Bradford, Judith Christian-Carter,
Lynda Macdonald and Paul Tew

✱ Croner-i
HR · Tax · H&S · Audit & Accounting

Croner-i Ltd
240 Blackfriars Road
London SE1 8NW
Tel: 0844 561 8166

Published by
Croner-i Ltd
240 Blackfriars Road
London SE1 8NW
Tel: 0844 561 8166

First published January 1984
Third Edition 1996
Fourth Edition 1997
Fifth Edition 1998
Sixth Edition 1999
Seventh Edition 2000
Eighth Edition 2001
Ninth Edition 2002
Tenth Edition 2003
Eleventh Edition 2004
Twelfth Edition 2005
Thirteenth Edition 2006
Fourteenth Edition 2007
Fifteenth Edition 2008
Sixteenth Edition 2009
Seventeenth Edition 2010
Eighteenth Edition 2011
Nineteenth Edition 2012
Twentieth Edition 2013
Twenty-first Edition 2014
Twenty-second Edition 2015
Twenty-third Edition 2016
Twenty-fourth Edition 2017
Twenty-fifth Edition 2018
© Croner-i Ltd

Crown copyright material is reproduced under the terms of the Open Government Licence. Although great care has been taken in the compilation and preparation of this work to ensure accuracy, the publishers cannot in any circumstances accept responsibility for any errors or omissions.

Subscribers to this book should be aware that only Acts of Parliament and Statutory Instruments have the force of law and that only the courts can authoritatively interpret the law.

ISBN 978-1-78887-116-7

Printed by Ovimex B.V. — The Netherlands

PREFACE

Key Rates and Data: Employment is a distillation of the most important information you need in the day-to-day running of your organisation. It will provide you with the facts and figures you need at your fingertips.

Key Rates and Data: Employment is supplied to subscribers as an element of the *Reference Book for Employers* service. We hope that you find it useful.

May 2018

Contents

CHAPTER 1

Payroll Data

Statutory Sick Pay

Statutory sick pay (SSP) is paid by an employer to a sick employee for up to 28 weeks. It provides a fixed weekly amount of benefit to the employee.

Weekly Rates of SSP

Tax year	Lower earnings limit	SSP
2018/19	£116.00	£92.05
2017/18	£113.00	£89.35
2016/17	£112.00	£88.45
2015/16	£112.00	£88.45
2014/15	£111.00	£87.55
2013/14	£109.00	£86.70
2012/13	£107.00	£85.85
2011/12	£102.00	£81.60

SMP, SPP and SAP

Statutory Maternity Pay

Statutory maternity pay (SMP) provides eligible women employees with up to 39 weeks' paid leave around the period of childbirth. The first six weeks are paid at 90% of average earnings; the remaining weeks are at the lower of 90% of earnings and a set rate. All employees are then entitled to a further 13 weeks of unpaid leave if they have not resumed work.

Set Rates of SMP

Tax year	Set rate
From 1 April 2018	£145.18
From 2 April 2017	£140.98
From 3 April 2016	£139.58
From 5 April 2015	£139.58
From 6 April 2014	£138.18
From 7 April 2013	£136.78
From 1 April 2012	£135.45
From 3 April 2011	£128.73

An employer may reclaim some or all of the SMP from the State. Only 92% of SMP may be recovered, except in the case of small employers who may recover over 100% of SMP. The compensation percentage is intended to compensate for the fact that SMP is subject to employer's National Insurance. Small employers are employers whose total PAYE and NIC bill for the previous year does not exceed the small employer relief threshold.

Compensation Percentages

Tax year	Compensation percentages
2011/12 and later	3.0%
Up to 2010/11	4.5%

Small Employers' Relief Threshold

Tax year	Small employers' relief threshold
From 2006 to present	£45,000

Statutory Paternity Pay

Statutory paternity pay (SPP) is payable for two weeks to employees who meet the qualifying conditions. It is payable at the lower of 90% of the employee's average weekly earnings and the set rate.

Set Rates of SPP

Tax year	Set rate
From 1 April 2018	£145.18
From 2 April 2017	£140.98
From 3 April 2016	£139.58
From 5 April 2015	£139.58
From 6 April 2014	£138.18
From 7 April 2013	£136.78
From 1 April 2012	£135.45
From 3 April 2011	£128.73

Statutory Adoption Pay

Statutory adoption pay (SAP) is payable to employees who adopt a child provided that the qualifying conditions are met. SAP provides most employees who adopt a child with up to 39 weeks' paid leave around the time of adoption. If the child is adopted by a couple, one may claim SAP and the other may claim statutory paternity pay (SPP). SAP is paid at a set rate, or 90% of average weekly earnings if these are less than the set rate of SAP. It is paid at a higher rate of 90% of average weekly earnings for the first six weeks.

3

Set Rates of SAP

Tax year	Set rate
From 1 April 2018	£145.18
From 2 April 2017	£140.98
From 3 April 2016	£139.58
From 5 April 2015	£139.58
From 6 April 2014	£138.18
From 7 April 2013	£136.78
From 1 April 2012	£135.45
From 3 April 2011	£128.73

Redundancy Pay

The amount of redundancy pay depends on the employee's length of service, subject to a minimum of two years and a maximum of 20 years. For each year's service the employee receives a portion of a week's wages according to his or her age that year. All continuous service from age 16 is reckonable. The proportion according to age is as shown in the following table.

Portion of a Week's Wages

Age	Portion of week's wages
under 21	half
22 to 40	one
41 and over	one and a half

The week's wages are subject to a statutory maximum amount, depending on when the employee was made redundant. This statutory maximum is now index-linked.

Maximum Week's Pay

Period	Maximum week's pay
From 6 April 2018	£508
From 6 April 2017 until 5 April 2018	£489
From 6 April 2016 until 5 April 2017	£479
From 6 April 2015 until 5 April 2016	£475
From 6 April 2014 until 5 April 2015	£464
From 1 February 2013 until 5 April 2014	£450
From 1 February 2012 until 31 January 2013	£430
From 1 February 2011 until 31 January 2012	£400

Northern Ireland Increase of Limits

Provision	From 22 March 2015	From 14 February 2016
Maximum amount of a week's pay	£490	£500
Limit on amount of compensatory award for unfair dismissal	£78,400	£79,100
Daily Rate for Guarantee Pay	£25.60	£25.90

Redundancy Pay Ready Reckoner for Redundancies on or after 1 October 2006

Age	Years of service																			
	2	3	4	5	6	7	8	9	10	11	12	13	14	15	16	17	18	19	20
17*	1																		
18	1	$1^{1/2}$																	
19	1	$1^{1/2}$	2																
20	1	$1^{1/2}$	2	$2^{1/2}$															
21	1	$1^{1/2}$	2	$2^{1/2}$	3														
22	1	$1^{1/2}$	2	$2^{1/2}$	3	$3^{1/2}$													
23	$1^{1/2}$	2	$2^{1/2}$	3	$3^{1/2}$	4	$4^{1/2}$												

PAYROLL DATA

Age	Years of service																		
24	2	$2^{1/2}$	3	$3^{1/2}$	4	$4^{1/2}$	5	$5^{1/2}$											
25	2	3	$3^{1/2}$	4	$4^{1/2}$	5	$5^{1/2}$	6	$6^{1/2}$										
26	2	3	4	$4^{1/2}$	5	$5^{1/2}$	6	$6^{1/2}$	7	$7^{1/2}$									
27	2	3	4	5	$5^{1/2}$	6	$6^{1/2}$	7	$7^{1/2}$	8	$8^{1/2}$								
28	2	3	4	5	6	$6^{1/2}$	7	$7^{1/2}$	8	$8^{1/2}$	9	$9^{1/2}$							
29	2	3	4	5	6	7	$7^{1/2}$	8	$8^{1/2}$	9	$9^{1/2}$	10	$10^{1/2}$						
30	2	3	4	5	6	7	8	$8^{1/2}$	9	$9^{1/2}$	10	$10^{1/2}$	11	$11^{1/2}$					
31	2	3	4	5	6	7	8	9	$9^{1/2}$	10	$10^{1/2}$	11	$11^{1/2}$	12	$12^{1/2}$				
32	2	3	4	5	6	7	8	9	10	$10^{1/2}$	11	$11^{1/2}$	12	$12^{1/2}$	13	$13^{1/2}$			
33	2	3	4	5	6	7	8	9	10	11	$11^{1/2}$	12	$12^{1/2}$	13	$13^{1/2}$	14	$14^{1/2}$		
34	2	3	4	5	6	7	8	9	10	11	12	$12^{1/2}$	13	$13^{1/2}$	14	$14^{1/2}$	15	$15^{1/2}$	
35	2	3	4	5	6	7	8	9	10	11	12	13	$13^{1/2}$	14	$14^{1/2}$	15	$15^{1/2}$	16	$16^{1/2}$
36	2	3	4	5	6	7	8	9	10	11	12	13	14	$14^{1/2}$	15	$15^{1/2}$	16	$16^{1/2}$	17
37	2	3	4	5	6	7	8	9	10	11	12	13	14	15	$15^{1/2}$	16	$16^{1/2}$	17	$17^{1/2}$
38	2	3	4	5	6	7	8	9	10	11	12	13	14	15	16	$16^{1/2}$	17	$17^{1/2}$	18
39	2	3	4	5	6	7	8	9	10	11	12	13	14	15	16	17	$17^{1/2}$	18	$18^{1/2}$
40	2	3	4	5	6	7	8	9	10	11	12	13	14	15	16	17	18	$18^{1/2}$	19
41	2	3	4	5	6	7	8	9	10	11	12	13	14	15	16	17	18	19	$19^{1/2}$
42	$2^{1/2}$	$3^{1/2}$	$4^{1/2}$	$5^{1/2}$	$6^{1/2}$	$7^{1/2}$	$8^{1/2}$	$9^{1/2}$	$10^{1/2}$	$11^{1/2}$	$12^{1/2}$	$13^{1/2}$	$14^{1/2}$	$15^{1/2}$	$16^{1/2}$	$17^{1/2}$	$18^{1/2}$	$19^{1/2}$	$20^{1/2}$
43	3	4	5	6	7	8	9	10	11	12	13	14	15	16	17	18	19	20	21
44	3	$4^{1/2}$	$5^{1/2}$	$6^{1/2}$	$7^{1/2}$	$8^{1/2}$	$9^{1/2}$	$10^{1/2}$	$11^{1/2}$	$12^{1/2}$	$13^{1/2}$	$14^{1/2}$	$15^{1/2}$	$16^{1/2}$	$17^{1/2}$	$18^{1/2}$	$19^{1/2}$	$20^{1/2}$	$21^{1/2}$
45	3	$4^{1/2}$	6	7	8	9	10	11	12	13	14	15	16	17	18	19	20	21	22
46	3	$4^{1/2}$	6	$7^{1/2}$	$8^{1/2}$	$9^{1/2}$	$10^{1/2}$	$11^{1/2}$	$12^{1/2}$	$13^{1/2}$	$14^{1/2}$	$15^{1/2}$	$16^{1/2}$	$17^{1/2}$	$18^{1/2}$	$19^{1/2}$	$20^{1/2}$	$21^{1/2}$	$22^{1/2}$
47	3	$4^{1/2}$	6	$7^{1/2}$	9	10	11	12	13	14	15	16	17	18	19	20	21	22	23
48	3	$4^{1/2}$	6	$7^{1/2}$	9	$10^{1/2}$	$11^{1/2}$	$12^{1/2}$	$13^{1/2}$	$14^{1/2}$	$15^{1/2}$	$16^{1/2}$	$17^{1/2}$	$18^{1/2}$	$19^{1/2}$	$20^{1/2}$	$21^{1/2}$	$22^{1/2}$	$23^{1/2}$
49	3	$4^{1/2}$	6	$7^{1/2}$	9	$10^{1/2}$	12	13	14	15	16	17	18	19	20	21	22	23	24
50	3	$4^{1/2}$	6	$7^{1/2}$	9	$10^{1/2}$	12	$13^{1/2}$	$14^{1/2}$	$15^{1/2}$	$16^{1/2}$	$17^{1/2}$	$18^{1/2}$	$19^{1/2}$	$20^{1/2}$	$21^{1/2}$	$22^{1/2}$	$23^{1/2}$	$24^{1/2}$
51	3	$4^{1/2}$	6	$7^{1/2}$	9	$10^{1/2}$	12	$13^{1/2}$	15	16	17	18	19	20	21	22	23	24	25
52	3	$4^{1/2}$	6	$7^{1/2}$	9	$10^{1/2}$	12	$13^{1/2}$	15	$16^{1/2}$	$17^{1/2}$	$18^{1/2}$	$19^{1/2}$	$20^{1/2}$	$21^{1/2}$	$22^{1/2}$	$23^{1/2}$	$24^{1/2}$	$25^{1/2}$
53	3	$4^{1/2}$	6	$7^{1/2}$	9	$10^{1/2}$	12	$13^{1/2}$	15	$16^{1/2}$	18	19	20	21	22	23	24	25	26
54	3	$4^{1/2}$	6	$7^{1/2}$	9	$10^{1/2}$	12	$13^{1/2}$	15	$16^{1/2}$	18	$19^{1/2}$	$20^{1/2}$	$21^{1/2}$	$22^{1/2}$	$23^{1/2}$	$24^{1/2}$	$25^{1/2}$	$26^{1/2}$
55	3	$4^{1/2}$	6	$7^{1/2}$	9	$10^{1/2}$	12	$13^{1/2}$	15	$16^{1/2}$	18	$19^{1/2}$	21	22	23	24	25	26	27

Age	Years of service																	
56	3	$4^{1/2}$ 6	$7^{1/2}$ 9	$10^{1/2}$12	$13^{1/2}$15	$16^{1/2}$18	$19^{1/2}$21	$22^{1/2}$ $23^{1/2}$ $24^{1/2}$ $25^{1/2}$ $26^{1/2}$ $27^{1/2}$
57	3	$4^{1/2}$ 6	$7^{1/2}$ 9	$10^{1/2}$12	$13^{1/2}$15	$16^{1/2}$18	$19^{1/2}$21	$22^{1/2}$24	25	26	27	28
58	3	$4^{1/2}$ 6	$7^{1/2}$ 9	$10^{1/2}$12	$13^{1/2}$15	$16^{1/2}$18	$19^{1/2}$21	$22^{1/2}$24	$25^{1/2}$ $26^{1/2}$ $27^{1/2}$ $28^{1/2}$
59	3	$4^{1/2}$ 6	$7^{1/2}$ 9	$10^{1/2}$12	$13^{1/2}$15	$16^{1/2}$18	$19^{1/2}$21	$22^{1/2}$24	$25^{1/2}$27	28	29
60	3	$4^{1/2}$ 6	$7^{1/2}$ 9	$10^{1/2}$12	$13^{1/2}$15	$16^{1/2}$18	$19^{1/2}$21	$22^{1/2}$24	$25^{1/2}$27	$28^{1/2}$ $29^{1/2}$
61**3	$4^{1/2}$ 6	$7^{1/2}$ 9	$10^{1/2}$12	$13^{1/2}$15	$16^{1/2}$18	$19^{1/2}$21	$22^{1/2}$24	$25^{1/2}$27	$28^{1/2}$30

* The table starts at age 17, as it is possible for a 17-year-old to have 2 years' service. Compulsory school leaving age can be 15¾ or 15⅘ where a child is 16 before 1 September. Particular care should be taken when calculating an individual's redundancy pay when they joined as an employee below the age of 16.

** The table stops at age 61 because, for employees age 61 and over, the payment remains the same as for age 61.

(Source: Department for Business, Enterprise and Regulatory Reform)

Guarantee Pay

An employee is entitled to a guaranteed payment for any day for which he or she is required to work but for which no work is provided. The employee is entitled to a maximum of five such payments in any three-month period. The daily rate is now index-linked.

Daily Rate for Guarantee Pay

Period	Daily rate
From 6 April 2018	£28.00
From 6 April 2017 until 5 April 2018	£27.00
From 6 April 2016 until 5 April 2017	£26.00
From 6 April 2015 until 5 April 2016	£26.00
From 6 April 2014 until 5 April 2015	£25.00
From 1 February 2013 until 5 April 2014	£24.20
From 1 February 2012 until 31 January 2013	£23.50
From 1 February 2011 until 31 January 2012	£22.20
From 1 February 2010 until 31 January 2011	£21.20

National Minimum Wage

The National Minimum Wage (NMW) rates are split into five levels depending on age and whether the employee is undergoing a formal apprenticeship. The rates are shown in the table below.

NMW			
Category	From 1 October 2016	From 1 April 2017	From 1 April 2018
National Living Wage (25 years and older)	£7.20	£7.50	£7.83
Main rate (21–24 years only)	£6.95	£7.05	£7.38
Development rate (18–20 years only)	£5.55	£5.60	£5.90
Youth rate (16–17)	£4.00	£4.05	£4.20
Apprentices currently exempt from the NMW (eg those under the age of 19 and older apprentices in the first year of apprenticeship)	£3.40	£3.50	£3.70

The *accommodation offset* rates are currently £7.00 per day and a weekly maximum of £49.00 from 1 April 2018.

Unfair Dismissal Limits

Compensation for unfair dismissal comprises up to three elements:
• basic award
• compensatory award
• additional award.

Basic Awards

The basic award has an upper limit based on redundancy pay. There is a minimum award if the dismissal was automatically unfair.

Limits on Basic Awards

Period	Minimum limit if automatically unfair	Upper limit
From 6 April 2018	£6203	£15,240
From 6 April 2017 until 5 April 2018	£5970	£14,670
From 6 April 2016 until 5 April 2017	£5853	£14,370
From 6 April 2015 until 5 April 2016	£5807	£14,250
From 6 April 2014 until 5 April 2015	£5676	£13,920
From 1 February 2013 until 5 April 2014	£5500	£13,500
From 1 February 2012 until 31 January 2013	£5300	£12,900
From 1 February 2011 until 31 January 2012	£5000	£12,000

Compensatory Award

The compensatory award itself comprises four elements:
  (a) estimated loss of wages to date of hearing
  (b) estimated future loss of earnings
  (c) loss of benefits and rights
  (d) loss of statutory rights.

Effective from 29 July 2013, compensation is the *lower* of a year's salary or the figures indicated below.

Compensation remains unlimited in certain types of claim, eg discrimination.

9

Compensatory Award

Period	Limit (or one year's salary — see above)
From 6 April 2018	£83,682
From 6 April 2017 until 5 April 2018	£80,541
From 6 April 2016 until 5 April 2017	£78,962
From 6 April 2015 until 5 April 2016	£78,335
From 6 April 2014 until 5 April 2015	£76,574
From 1 February 2013 until 5 April 2014	£74,200
From 1 February 2012 until 31 January 2013	£72,300
From 1 February 2011 until 31 January 2012	£68,400

Additional Award

The additional award (of between 26 and 52 weeks' pay) is made if an employer refuses to obey an order to reinstate or re-engage the employee without good reason.

The week's pay is limited to the same maximum as redundancy pay, currently £508.

CHAPTER 2

Income Tax Data

Rates of Income Tax

Income tax is assessed on slices of taxable income at varying rates.

"Taxable income" is, broadly, all income, grossed up when appropriate, less reliefs, allowances and other deductions.

For 2015/16, dividends otherwise taxable at the 20% basic rate were taxed at the 10% dividend ordinary rate and dividends otherwise taxable at the 40% higher rate were taxable at the 32.5% dividend upper rate. Dividends otherwise taxable at the 45% additional higher rate were taxable at the 37.5% dividend additional rate.

Where income fell within the basic rate band, the 10% dividend tax credit (which reduced the amount of tax paid on income from shares) extinguished any liability. From 6 April 2016, the 10% dividend tax credit was abolished and replaced by a new £5000 tax-free dividend allowance on dividend income for all taxpayers. The dividend allowance applies to dividends received from UK resident and non-UK resident companies.

For 2016/17 and 2017/18, UK residents pay tax on any dividends received over the £5000 allowance at the following three tax rates — 7.5% for basic rate taxpayers, 32.5% for higher rate taxpayers and 38.1% for additional rate taxpayers. This was an increase of 7.5% where dividend income exceeds £5000. Dividends paid within pensions and ISAs remain tax-free and unaffected by these changes. The dividend allowance and tax rates remained unchanged for tax year 2017/18. For 2018/19, the tax-free dividend allowance was reduced from £5000 to £2000, but the three dividend tax rates remain unchanged.

From 6 April 2015, the 10% savings tax rate was abolished and the band of savings income that is subject to the 0% rate extended to £5000.

The starting rate limit was not subject to indexation in 2015/16 and the 0% savings band income limit has remained set at £5000 for 2016/17 onwards and applies across the whole of the UK.

From 6 April 2016 onwards, a personal savings allowance removes tax on up to £1000 of savings income for basic rate taxpayers and up to £500 for higher rate taxpayers. For 2018/19, a basic rate taxpayer does not have to pay tax on interest if their taxable income is less than £17,850 (ie £11,850 + £1000 + £5000).

From 2010/11 the personal allowance was progressively withdrawn from those with adjusted net income in excess of £100,000, at the rate of £1 per £2 of excess income.

Personal Allowances

Every taxpayer, including a spouse or civil partner, is entitled to a personal allowance, regardless of age. The married couple's allowance can now only be claimed where either spouse was born before 6 April 1935.

For 2018/19, the married couple's allowance is subject to an income limit of £28,900, whereby the allowance is reduced by £1 for every £2 of income received over this limit, until it reaches the minimum amount, set at £3360, below which it cannot fall.

Personal Allowances

Tax year	Personal Allowance	Married Couple's Allowance
2018/19	£11,850	£3360
2017/18	£11,500	£3260
2016/17	£11,000	£3220
2015/16	£10,600	£3220
2014/15	£10,000	£3140
2013/14	£9440	£3040
2012/13	£8105	£2960
2011/12	£7475	£2800

*National

Annual Rates of Income Tax

Tax year	Taxable Income	Rate	Cumulative Tax
2018/19	£0–34,500	20%	£6900.00
	£34,501–£150,000	40%	£46,200.00
	Over £150,000	45%	—
2017/18	£0–£33,500	20%	£6700.00
	£33,501–£150,000	40%	£46,600.00
	Over £150,000 (Starting rate and limit for savings income Nil%, £5000)	45%	—
For 2017/18, the income tax bands for Scottish taxpayers are set at a different level than the rest of the UK. For Scottish taxpayers, the basic rate limit is £31,930	£0–£31,930	20%	£6386.00
	£31,931–£150,000	40%	£47,228.00
	Over £150,000 A Scottish taxpayer is an individual whose only or main place of residence is in Scotland or is a Scottish Parliamentarian	45%	—
2016/17	£1 to £32,000	20%	£6400.00
	£32,001 to £150,000	40%	£53,600.00
	Over £150,000 (Starting rate and limit for savings income £5000)	45%	—
2015/16	£1 to £31,785	20%	£6357.00
	£31,786 to £150,000	40%	£53,642.60
	Over £150,000 (Starting rate and limit for savings income £5000)	45%	—
2014/15	£0–£31,865	20%	£6373.00
	£31,866– £150,000	40%	£53,626.60
	Over £150,000 (Starting rate limit for savings income £2880)	45%	—

Tax year	Taxable Income	Rate	Cumulative Tax
2013/14	£0–£32,010	20%	£6402.00
	£32,011–£150,000	40%	£53,598.00
	Over £150,000 (Starting rate limit for savings income £2790)	45%	—
2012/13	£0–£34,370	20%	£6874.00
	£34,371–£150,000	40%	£53,126.00
	Over £150,000	50%	—
2011/12	£1–£35,000	20%	£7000.00
	£35,001–£150,000	40%	£53,000.00
	Over £150,000	50%	—

From 2018/19, Scotland will for the first time have both different income tax thresholds and two additional income tax bands when compared to the rest of the UK.

Tax year	Scottish Income Tax Rates	Scottish Tax Bands	Cumulative Tax
2018/19	Scottish starter rate 19%	£0–£200	£380.00
	Scottish basic rate 20%	£2001–£12,150	£2030.00
	Scottish intermediate rate 21%	£12,151–£31,580	£4080.30
	Scottish higher rate 41%	£31,581–£150,000	£48,552.20
	Scottish additional rate 46%	Over £150,000	—

Scottish taxpayer broadly means those individuals whose only or main place of residence is in Scotland or who is a Scottish Parliamentarian.

Age Allowances

From 6 April 2016, there is a single personal allowance, regardless of a person's age. The married couple's allowance is now only due if at least one spouse or civil partner was born before 6 April 1935, ie aged 82 or over. From 2010/11, there is only one married couple's age-related allowance, with relief given at a rate of 10%. The allowance is subject to the same income restriction as the age-related personal allowance and can be reduced down to a minimum level.

Age Allowances

Tax year	Single 65–74	Single 75+	Married 65–74	Married 75+	Income limit
2018/19	N/A****	N/A****	N/A****	£8695	£28,900
2017/18	N/A***	N/A***	N/A*	£8445	£28,000
2016/17	N/A****	N/A****	N/A*	£8355	£27,700
2015/16	N/A****	£10,660***	N/A*	£8355	£27,700
2014/15	£10,500**	£10,660***	N/A*	£8165	£27,000
2013/14	£10,500**	£10,660***	N/A*	£7915	£26,100
2012/13	£10,500	£10,660	N/A*	£7705	£25,400
2011/12	£9940	£10,090	N/A*	£7295	£24,000

*As the married couple's allowance is only available if at least one spouse or civil partner was born before 6 April 1935, at least one must be aged 75+ for 2009/10 onwards (only available if the individual was born before 6 April 1948).
**Only available if the individual was born before 6 April 1948.
***Only available if the individual was born before 6 April 1938.
****No longer available as the basic personal allowance is higher.

Other Allowances

Blind Person's Allowance

This is paid to a taxpayer who is registered as blind for any part of the tax year, at the following rates.

Blind Person's Allowance

Tax years	Allowance
2018/19	£2390
2017/18	£2320
2016/17	£2290
2015/16	£2290
2014/15	£2230
2013/14	£2160
2012/13	£2100
2011/12	£1980

Dividend Allowance and Personal Savings Allowance

These allowances have been introduced in 2016/17. They exempt the first slice of dividend income and savings income from tax, but the income is still included in the computation when ascertaining in which tax band other income falls.

The dividend allowance is £5000 and is available to all taxpayers.

The dividend allowance was reduced to £2000 from 2018/19.

The personal savings allowance is £1000 for basic rate taxpayers and £500 for higher rate taxpayers. It is not available to additional rate taxpayers.

Life Assurance Relief

Life assurance relief was available for policies taken out before 14 March 1984 which met certain conditions. The relief had been 12.5% of premiums since 6 April 1989 but has been abolished from 6 April 2015.

Taxation of Company Cars

The Percentage Basis

A company car's value for tax purposes is assessed as a percentage of its list price.

The percentage of list price depends on the level of carbon dioxide emissions, and generally ranges up to 37% (35% before 2015/16). There is no reduction for older cars.

The CO_2 emissions figure (in grams per kilometre) for cars registered on or after 1 March 2001 is recorded on the vehicle registration document. For cars registered between 1 January 1998 and 28 February 2001, the emissions figure can be ascertained from a database maintained by the Society of Motor Manufacturers and Traders (*www.smmt.co.uk*), or may be found on an EU certificate of conformity. Where more than one figure is given, the relevant figure is the combined figure, but where a car is a dual-fuel car, the lower emissions figure is taken.

The appropriate percentage for the very few cars with an internal combustion engine and one or more reciprocating pistons but without an approved CO_2 emissions figure is based on their engine size, as follows.

Cylinder capacity of a car in cubic centimetres	Appropriate percentage 2015/16	Appropriate percentage 2016/17	Appropriate percentage 2017/18	Appropriate percentage 2018/19
1400 or less	15%	16%	18%	20%
More than 1400 but no more than 2000	25%	27%	29%	31%
More than 2000	37%	37%	37%	37%

The appropriate percentage for every car first registered before 1 January 1998 is based on its engine size, even if (exceptionally) it has an approved CO_2 emissions figure.

Cylinder capacity of a car in cubic centimetres	Appropriate percentage 2015/16	Appropriate percentage 2016/17	Appropriate percentage 2017/18	Appropriate percentage 2018/19
1400 or less	15%	16%	18%	20%
More than 1400 but no more than 2000	22%	27%	29%	31%
More than 2000	32%	37%	37%	37%

The appropriate percentage for diesel cars registered on or after 1 January 1998 is increased by adding a further three percentage point supplement to the appropriate percentage up to the 37% maximum. From 6 April 2018, the diesel supplement rate will be increased from 3% to 4%.

List Price

List price is the price published by the car's manufacturer, importer or distributor as the inclusive price for a single car of that type on an open market retail sale in the UK, and the list price to be taken is that applying on the day immediately before the date of the car's first registration.

Cars without an actual list price will be taxed on a notional list price basis.

The following items are included in the car's list price:

- delivery charges
- VAT
- car tax (abolished for cars first supplied after 12 November 1992)
- customs and import duties
- standard accessories fitted when the car was supplied
- optional accessories fitted after the car was first supplied and which cost over £100
- replacement accessories which are superior to the originals
- adaptations for the disabled, if made before 6 April 1995
- basic number plates.

The following items are not included in the list price:

- running costs such as petrol, road tax, AA membership, etc
- warranties
- telephones
- optional accessories costing less than £100 fitted after the car was supplied
- replacement accessories of the same standard as the originals
- adaptations for the disabled made after 5 April 1995
- from 6 April 1998, any element of the list price or cost of accessories directly related to enabling the car to run on road fuel gases
- personalised number plates
- from 6 April 2011 relevant security features provided to meet a physical threat to the employee arising from the nature of the employment.

A car which is more than 15 years old at the end of the tax year and has an open market value of at least £15,000, ie a "classic car", is assessed at its open market value if this is greater than the list price.

Prior to 2011/12 the list price used for calculating taxable benefit was capped at £80,000. From 6 April 2011, this figure is no longer limited to £80,000. The list price may be reduced by up to £5000 if the employee makes a contribution to the capital cost.

Reductions in Charge

The tax charge for a company car is reduced *pro rata* if the car is not available for the whole year. Periods of less than 30 days during which the car is unavailable (eg for repairs) are disregarded.

The taxable value of a company car is reduced by any amount which the employee pays to the employer for the private use of the car.

Car Fuel Benefit

If an employee is provided with fuel by the employer, the employee is liable to a further tax charge on the value of the fuel. From 2003/04 onwards the charge is linked to the carbon dioxide emissions of the car. It is calculated by multiplying a statutory figure by the percentage used to calculate the car benefit.

Tax year	Statutory figure
2018/19	23,400
2017/18	£22,600
2016/17	£22,200
2015/16	£22,100
2014/15	£21,700
2013/14	£21,100
2012/13	£20,200
2011/12	£18,800

Taxable Benefits from Employment

Most benefits provided to an employee in consequence of his or her employment are taxable. The general rule is given below but many benefits are now subject to specific rules, summarised in the following table.

Taxable Benefits

Benefit	Amount assessable
Accommodation	Unless exempt as representative accommodation, the higher of the actual rent paid by the employer or the rateable value or agreed equivalent on accommodation valued up to £75,000 (including lower-paid employees for 2015/16 and earlier).
Accommodation, expensive	If the property costs more than £75,000: the excess over £75,000 multiplied by the official interest rate at the start of the tax year (including lower-paid employees for 2015/16 and earlier).
Asset, gift of	If new, the cost of the asset for P11D employees. If used by the employee, the higher of the market value, or the market value when first used less benefit assessed for personal use. For 2015/16 and earlier, second-hand value for a lower-paid employee.
Asset, personal use of	20% of the asset's market value.
Beneficial loan	Unless exempt, the amount by which interest paid is less than that using the official rate of interest.
Chauffeur, nanny, etc	Total cost of employing that person (including employer's National Insurance).
Childcare facilities	Unless exempt, the share of the full cost of facilities.
Clothing	See Assets above.
Company car	Percentage of list price.

Benefit	Amount assessable
Company van	Scale charge of £3350 (£3230 for 2017/18, £3170 for 2016/17, £3150 for 2015/16, £3090 for 2014/15, £3000 for 2013/14 and earlier) with an additional scale charge of £633 for private use fuel (£610 for 2017/18, £598 for 2016/17, £594 for 2015/16, £581 for 2014/15, £564 for 2013/14 and £550 for 2010/11–2012/13. There is no tax charge where private use is insignificant or the van is only used privately for commuting to and from work.
Employer's own products or services	The marginal cost of providing the product or service.
Fuel for company car	Percentage of statutory figure.
Medical insurance	Premiums paid.
Membership of clubs	Subscription to the club.
Mobile telephone	Unless exempt (see Tax-free Benefits (*https://app.croneri.co.uk/key-rates-and-data/income-tax-data?product=3#DCAM-1169047*)), cost of rental and calls, and use of handset.
Scholarships	Cost, with a few exceptions.
Share options and similar	See Option schemes and similar.
Travel	Usually cost, unless a tax deductible business expense.
Vouchers exchanged for cash	Full face value (including lower-paid employees for 2015/16 and earlier).
Vouchers, gift	Cost to employer of providing the voucher (including lower-paid employees for 2015/16 and earlier).

The following benefits are tax-free, provided certain conditions are met.

Tax-free Benefits

Benefit	Conditions to be tax-free
Beneficial loan	Any one of: • the loan is less than £10,000 (£5000 for 2013/14 and earlier) • the loan is given by an employer who is in the business of making loans and it is on the same terms as offered to the public • the loan is a qualifying advance of business expenses • the loan is to buy into a trading partnership or close company.
Canteen facilities	The same facilities are available to all employees. The exemption does not apply from 2011/12 if the facilities are provided under a salary sacrifice scheme.
Car parking	At or near the place of work.
Chauffeur	If used on the organisation's business only.
Childcare facilities	Facilities must be provided or arranged by the employer and comply with certain conditions and local authority regulations. From 6 April 2005 the provision of other approved childcare or childcare vouchers is exempt up to a weekly limit (£55 per week for 2006/07 onwards. For employees who first received the approved childcare or childcare vouchers in 2011/12 onwards, the weekly limit for basic rate taxpayers is £55, higher rate taxpayers is £28 and for additional rate taxpayers is £25 (£22 for 2011/13).
Christmas/other parties	Cost does not exceed £150 per person per year.

Benefit	Conditions to be tax-free
Clothes	Uniform, safety clothing or bearing the organisation's logo.
Company pool car	Use of a pool car only for the organisation's business.
Education, full time	All of the following conditions must be met: • the course must last at least one academic year • the employee must maintain attendance of 20 weeks a year • the amount must not exceed £15,480.
Entertainment	Incidental to employment duties.
Gift	Unrelated to employment or not from the employer and not worth more than £250 a year.
Green travel	Including travel to work on works buses (minimum of nine seats), cycles and cycle safety equipment provided for travel to work, and up to 5 April 2013, cyclists' breakfasts on designated "cycle to work" days.
Hotel bills	Necessary food and accommodation where the travel is qualifying for tax relief and £5 a day personal expenses in the UK and £10 a day overseas while travelling overnight on business.
Housing	Necessary to perform duty properly, customary for that employment, or necessary for security.
Laundry	Clothing qualifies for tax relief.
Liability insurance	But not cover for a criminal offence.
Long service awards	Service of at least 20 years. Award not to exceed £50 per year of service.
Medical check-ups	Routine medical check-ups to confirm fitness for work.

Benefit	Conditions to be tax-free
Medical insurance	Only for trips abroad on company business where the cost is reimbursed by the employer.
Mobile telephone	For all employees but restricted from 6 April 2006 to one phone per employee and not extended to members of the employee's family or household.
Outplacement counselling	Where employee is made redundant.
Pension contributions	Pension scheme is registered with HMRC.
Relocation	Qualifying expenses and benefits up to £8000.
Security measures	Necessary to protect an employee or his or her family and not comprising a vehicle or accommodation.
Share options	See Option schemes and similar.
Sports facilities	Provided by an employer in-house.
Suggestion schemes	Cash awards up to £5000 subject to meeting qualifying conditions.
Training costs	Related to an employee's work and meeting certain conditions.
Travel on business	When a proper business expense. Benchmark scale rates for subsistence payments are published by HMRC. They are: for 2016/17 onwards, £5 (5-hour rate, or £15 if ongoing after 8pm), £10 (10-hour rate or £20 if ongoing after 8pm), £25 (15-hour rate, extending after 8pm); previously breakfast rate £5; one-meal (five-hour) rate £5; two-meal (10-hour) rate £10; late evening-meal rate £15; maximum three meals per day.
Trivial benefits	From 6 April 2016, trivial benefits up to £50 where they are not provided as remuneration nor provided under a salary sacrifice scheme.

HMRC Authorised Mileage Rates

An employee who is reimbursed for the use of his or her own car on company business at the HMRC authorised mileage rate is regarded as having been compensated for his or her costs. The employee, therefore, is not liable to tax on the rate.

The use of the authorised mileage rates is on a statutory footing. If the mileage rate paid exceeds the authorised rate, the excess is taxable while, if the rate paid is lower, a claim for tax relief may be made for the shortfall as a business expense.

Employees can no longer claim the actual motoring costs involved in using their private vehicles for business travel.

Statutory Car Mileage Allowance

All cars and vans	Rate per mile	Passenger rate
Up to first 10,000 business miles	45p	5p
Additional business miles	25p	5p

A supplementary tax-free allowance of 5p per mile can be paid for each passenger (other than the driver) who is also an employee travelling on company business. This passenger allowance can also be paid when a company owned car or van is used.

HMRC also publishes authorised mileage rates for bicycles and motor bikes.

HMRC Authorised Mileage Rates for Bicycles and Motorbikes

Tax year	Bicycles	Motor Bikes
2002/03 onwards	20p	24p

Company Car Advisory Fuel Rates from 1 March 2018

HMRC has announced new advisory fuel rates that can be used by employers paying employees a business mileage when driving an employer-provided car. These rates can also be used when charging employees for fuel provided for private miles and ordinary commuting.

These rates apply to all journeys on or after 1 March 2018 until further notice. For one month from the date of change, employers may use either the previous or new current rates, as they choose. Employers may therefore make or require supplementary payments if they so wish, but are under no obligation to do either.

Engine size	Petrol	LPG
1400cc or less	11p (previously 11p)	7p (previously 7p)
1401cc to 2000cc	14p (previously 14p)	8p (previously 9p)
Over 2000cc	22p (previously 21p)	13p (previously 14p)

Engine size	Diesel
1600cc or less	9p (previously 9p)
1601cc to 2000cc	11p (previously 11p)
Over 2000cc	13p (previously 13p)

Official Interest Rates

The official rate of interest is used to determine the taxable benefit of a beneficial loan to an employee. The average balance of the loan is multiplied by the appropriate official rate for the period that the loan is outstanding. This is compared with any interest paid by the employee. If the interest paid is less than the amount calculated using the official rate, the difference is a taxable benefit assessable on the employee.

The official rate is also used to calculate the assessable benefit when an employee is provided with use of a living accommodation costing more than £75,000.

If a loan is outstanding for an entire tax year, the average balance may be multiplied by the average annual rate. The official rate of interest of 3.00% is revised downwards to 2.50% with effect from 6 April 2017.

Average Annual Rate

Tax year	Annual rate (%)
2015/16 to 2016/17	3.00
2014/15	3.25
2010/11 to 2013/14	4.00

Official Interest Rates (Overseas)

HMRC may prescribe a lower "official interest rate" for a loan made in a foreign currency to an employee who has lived in that country during the previous five years.

Overseas Interest Rates

Country	Currency	Tax year	Average annual rate (%)
Japan	yen	1995/96 onwards	3.9
Switzerland	franc	1995/96 onwards	5.5

Flat Rate Expense Allowances

Deductions from taxable income are allowed for tools, special clothing, etc purchased by employees and which the employer does not provide. Rather than claim all items of expense separately, certain employees may claim a flat rate.

Flat Rate Expense Allowances

Category of worker	Tax years 2008/09 onwards	2007/08 and earlier
Agriculture: all workers	£100	£70
Aluminium:		
most operators	£140	£130
cable hands, case makers, etc	£80	£60
apprentices	£60	£45
other workers	£120	£100
Banks:		
uniformed employees	£60	£45
Brass and copper:		
all workers	£120	£100

Category of worker	Tax years 2008/09 onwards	2007/08 and earlier
Buildings:		
joiners and carpenters	£140	£105
cement workers and roofers	£80	£55
labourers and navvies	£60	£45
other workers	£120	£85
Building materials:		
stone masons	£120	£85
tile makers and labourers	£60	£45
other workers	£80	£55
Clothing:		
lacemakers, hosiery bleachers, dyers, scourers and knitters	£60	£45
other workers	£60	£45
Constructional engineering:		
blacksmiths, burners, caulkers, chippers, drillers, erectors, fitters, holders up, markers off, platers, riggers, riveters, rivet heaters, scaffolders, sheeters, template workers, turners and welders	£140	£115
banksmen, labourers, shop helpers, slewers and straighteners	£80	£60
apprentices and storekeepers	£60	£45
other workers	£100	£75
Electrical and electricity supply:		
workers incurring laundry costs only	£60	£45
other workers	£120	£90

Category of worker	Tax years 2008/09 onwards	2007/08 and earlier
Engineering:		
pattern makers	£140	£120
labourers, supervisors and unskilled	£80	£60
apprentices and storekeepers	£60	£45
motor mechanics in repair shops	£120	£100
other workers	£120	£100
Fire service:		
uniformed fire fighters and fire officers	£80	£60
Food:		
all workers	£60	£45
Forestry:		
all workers	£100	£70
Glass:		
all workers	£80	£60
Healthcare:		
ambulance staff on active service	£140	£110
nurses, midwives, chiropodists, dental nurses, occupational, speech and other therapists, orthoptists, phlebotomists, physiotherapists, radiographers	£100	£70
plaster room orderlies, hospital porters, ward clerks, sterile supply workers, hospital domestics and catering staff	£100	£60
laboratory staff, pharmacists and pharmacy assistants, maintenance workers, ground staff and all other uniformed workers	£60	£45
uniformed ancillary staff: uniformed workers	£60	£45

Category of worker	Tax years 2008/09 onwards	2007/08 and earlier
Heating:		
pipe fitters and plumbers	£120	£100
coverers, laggers, domestic glaziers, heating engineers and their mates	£120	£90
gas workers and other workers	£100	£70
Iron and steel:		
day labourers, general labourers, stockmen, timekeepers, warehouse staff and weighmen	£80	£60
apprentices	£60	£45
other workers	£140	£120
Iron mining:		
fillers, miners and underground workers	£120	£100
other workers	£100	£75
Leather:		
curriers, fellmongering workers and tanning operatives	£80	£55
other workers	£60	£45
Particular engineering:		
pattern makers	£140	£120
chainmakers, cleaners, galvanisers, tinners, wire drawers and toolmakers in lockmaking industry	£120	£100
apprentices and storekeepers	£60	£45
other workers	£80	£60
Police force:		
uniformed officers to chief inspector	£140	£110

Category of worker	Tax years 2008/09 onwards	2007/08 and earlier
Precious metals:		
all workers	£100	£70
Printing:		
letterpress, electrical engineers, electrotypers, ink and roller makers, machine minders, maintenance engineers and stereotypers	£140	£105
benchhands, compositors, readers and section wireroom operators	£60	£45
other workers	£100	£70
Prisons:		
uniformed officers	£80	£55
Public service: docks		
dockers, dredgers, drivers and hopper steerers	£80	£55
other workers	£60	£45
Public service: transport		
garage hands	£80	£55
conductors and drivers	£60	£45
Quarrying:		
all workers	£100	£70
Railways:		
all workers except craftsmen	£100	£70
Seamen:		
carpenters (passenger liners)	£165	£135
carpenters (cargo, tankers, ferries)	£140	£130

Category of worker	Tax years 2008/09 onwards	2007/08 and earlier
Shipyards:		
blacksmiths, strikers, boiler makers, burners, carpenters, caulkers, drillers, furnacemen, holders up, fillers, platers, plumbers, riveters, sheet iron workers, shipwrights, tubers and welders	£140	£115
labourers	£80	£60
apprentices and storekeepers	£60	£45
other workers	£100	£70
Textiles and textile printing:		
carders, carding engineers, overlookers and technicians	£120	£85
other workers	£80	£60
Vehicles:		
builders, railway wagon repairers and makers	£140	£105
railway wagon painters and letterers, builders' and repairers' assistants	£80	£60
other workers	£60	£45
Wood and furniture:		
carpenters, cabinet makers, joiners, wood carvers and woodcutting machinists	£140	£115
organ builders and packing case makers	£120	£90
coopers, labourers, polishers and upholsterers	£60	£45
other workers	£100	£75

Employee Share Schemes

There are, broadly, four types of share scheme currently available to employees which have tax benefits attached to them. These are summarised in the following table.

Four Types of Share Scheme

Usual name	First introduced	Legislation	Current Limits
Company share option plan	1984	ss.521–526 and schedule 4 ITEPA 2003	£30,000
Savings-related option	1980	ss.516–520 and schedule 3 ITEPA 2003	£500 a month
Share Incentive Plan (formerly All-employee Share scheme)	2000	ss.488–515 and schedule 2 ITEPA 2003	£3600 (free shares); £1800 (partnership shares), but limited to salary; two matching shares for each partnership share
Enterprise management incentive scheme	2000	ss.527–541 and schedule 5 ITEPA 2003	£250,000 limit on the value of shares over which options may be held by an employee, £3 million (in total)

A company share plan within schedule 4 ITEPA 2003 qualifies to qualify for tax relief. Under such a plan no income tax is payable either when the option is granted or exercised. The plan allows directors and employees at some future date to buy shares in their company at the current price.

The rules of the plan are that:

- the option must be exercised between 3 and 10 years after it is granted; early exercise may be permitted in certain "clemency" conditions
- the maximum market value of shares over which an option can be granted is £30,000
- share options must be granted with an exercise price which is equal to or exceeds the market value of a share at the grant date; discounted options cannot be granted
- the option holder must be a director working at least 25 hours a week or employee of the company when the option is granted
- the shares must not be subject to any restrictions other than requiring their sale when the employment ends
- the option holder must not own more than 30% (25% before 17 July 2013) of the company's ordinary shares
- the option must be non-transferable
- the shares must meet certain conditions.

Profit-related Pay

Profit-related pay (PRP) allowed an employee to receive part of his or her pay free of tax to the extent that it was related to the profit of his or her employer. The relief has been phased out, and no relief is available for profit periods beginning on or after 1 January 2000. PRP remained subject to Class 1 NICs.

Relocation

An employer may provide up to £8000 tax-free to employees to help them and their families to relocate.

This may be used to pay for:

- legal fees and estate agents' fees in selling an existing home (although it is not necessary to sell an existing home to qualify for the tax-free payment)
- legal fees and stamp duty on buying a new home
- furniture removal
- travel and subsistence expenses while looking for new accommodation
- temporary accommodation at the new location
- new carpets, curtains and other items to replace those which are unsuitable for use in the new home
- bridging loans (with some restrictions)
- the services of a relocation organisation.

The limit may *not* be used to pay:
- compensation for moving to a more expensive area
- compensation for a loss in selling a previous house.

Termination Payments

The following payments for termination of employment are tax-free:
- statutory redundancy pay
- non-statutory redundancy pay up to £30,000
- lump sums paid to employees to compensate for loss of employment through disability, injury or ill health which prevents the employee carrying out the duties of the employment
- compensation for wrongful dismissal up to £30,000
- *ex-gratia* payments to certain overseas workers (see *Ex-gratia Payments to Overseas Workers*)
- lump sums paid on retirement or death from a pension scheme registered by HMRC, or an employer-financed retirement benefits scheme
- certain other termination payments to which the employee has no contractual entitlement up to £30,000.

The £30,000 Limit

In deciding whether the £30,000 termination payment limit has been reached, it is necessary to include:
- statutory redundancy pay (even though this is tax-free anyway)
- the value of any asset, such as a company car, transferred to the employee
- other payments relating to termination and not in the above list.

PAYE

PAYE Thresholds

	PAYE threshold		National Insurance lower earnings limit	
Tax year	Monthly	Weekly	Monthly	Weekly
2018/19	£988	£228	£503	£116
2017/18	£958	£221	£490	£113
2016/17	£917	£212	£486	£112

| Tax year | PAYE threshold | | National Insurance lower earnings limit | |
	Monthly	Weekly	Monthly	Weekly
2015/16	£833	£204	£486	£112
2014/15	£833	£192	£356	£82
2013/14	£786	£181	£473	£109
2012/13	£676	£156	£464	£107
2011/12	£623	£144	£442	£102

Quarterly Payments

PAYE may be paid to HMRC quarterly if the monthly remittances of PAYE and National Insurance do not exceed the following.

Quarterly Returns

From	Amount
6 April 2000	£1500

Taxed Award Scheme

An employer may make arrangements to pay the tax on a prize or award made to an employee under an incentive plan by using the Taxed Award Scheme (TAS). This may be used for higher rate taxpayers as well as those paying tax at the basic rate. The amount of the award must be grossed up in calculating the tax. Class 1 National Insurance is payable on the amount of tax paid under the TAS, and on the award if it is in the form of earnings (ie cash, vouchers, etc). If the award is in the form of goods, Class 1A NICs are due.

PAYE Settlement Agreements

A PAYE settlement agreement (PSA) is an arrangement which enables an employer to settle the employees' tax liabilities on certain benefits and expense payments in a single sum. Benefits and expenses covered are those which are minor or irregular, or where it is impracticable for PAYE to be operated.

Examples of items which may be included are:

- minor items
- personal incidental expenses on business trips which exceed the daily limit

- staff entertainment
- subscriptions
- relocation benefits and expenses in excess of the £8000 limit
- occasional use of a company flat
- shared use of taxis home
- shared use of company bus to work.

The employer must gross up the total amount to calculate the tax payable. The calculation must reflect the marginal rates of tax of the employees concerned, usually by reference to the actual employees.

NICs are payable annually by 19/22 October following the end of the tax year (by the employer only) under Class 1B on expenses and benefits covered by a PSA, which would otherwise be liable to Class 1 or Class 1A NICs, and on the tax payable.

From April 2018, the Government aims to reduce the administrative burden on employers specifically by lifting the current requirement on employers to renew their PSA annually by providing for an "enduring agreement" and ensuring the regulations allow for digitisation of the PSA process at a future stage. The Government is not proposing to amend the benefits or expenses which can be covered by a PSA.

Recovering Underpaid Tax through PAYE

Under self-assessment, income tax is paid in two instalments: on 31 January in the tax year and on the 31 July following. Any balance of tax is due on the 31 January following the tax year, although underpayments of less than £3000 may be collected through PAYE. HMRC replaced the single scale of £3000 by a graduated scale of limits. The new limits came into effect for 2015/16 and subsequent tax years, and are set as follows.

PAYE Graduated Scale of Limits

The expected amount of PAYE income of an employee in the tax year for which the code is determined	The total amount of debt that may be recovered from an employee in that tax year
Less than £30,000	No more than £3000
£30,000 or more but less than £40,000	No more than £5000

The expected amount of PAYE income of an employee in the tax year for which the code is determined	The total amount of debt that may be recovered from an employee in that tax year
£40,000 or more but less than £50,000	No more than £7000
£50,000 or more but less than £60,000	No more than £9000
£60,000 or more but less than £70,000	No more than £11,000
£70,000 or more but less than £80,000	No more than £13,000
£80,000 or more but less than £90,000	No more than £15,000
£90,000 or more	No more than £17,000

This protects those on lower incomes, with no change to the maximum of £3000 that could be coded out for those with earnings of less than £30,000 a year; and introduces a graduated, income-related scale for earnings of £30,000 or more so that a maximum of £17,000 could be coded out for a person with earnings of over £90,000. The coding out limit of £3000 for PAYE underpayments or self-assessment balancing payments continues, unless the taxpayer objects.

Interest on Late and Overpaid Tax

Where tax has been overpaid by the taxpayer, the repayment is accompanied by interest on overpaid tax, referred to as repayment supplement. The supplement itself is not taxable. Under self-assessment, the repayment supplement runs from the time the tax was paid until the repayment is made. Tax deducted at source, including under PAYE, is treated as if it had been paid on 31 January following the end of the tax year.

For late payments the interest now charged is the Bank of England base rate plus 2.5 and for overpayments, the interest rate is Bank of England base rate minus 1, with a minimum repayment rate of 0.5%, regardless of the Bank of England base rate.

The Bank of England Monetary Policy Committee cut the Bank of England base rate to 0.25% on 4 August 2016. As a result of the change in the base rate, HMRC interest rates for late payment were reduced to 2.75% from 23 August 2016.

The Bank of England Monetary Policy Committee voted on 2 November 2017 to increase the Bank of England base rate to 0.5%. As a consequence of the change in the base rate, HMRC interest rates for late payment are increased to 3%. Repayment interest rates remain unchanged at 0.5%.

Tax: Miscellaneous

Gift Aid

This is a system of donating to charities, which:
- provides tax relief for single gifts to charities
- may be used by companies or individuals
- may only be used for gifts of money, not goods or services.

To qualify as a Gift Aid payment, the donor should complete a Gift Aid declaration. The declaration may refer to specified donation(s) already made, or all donations made, or to be made, in a specified period. Gift Aid declarations may be made orally, in which case they are not effective unless the charity provides the donor with a written summary.

Payroll Giving

This scheme allows an employee to make contributions to charity by regular deductions from salary with tax relief at the employee's marginal tax rate given at source under PAYE. The contributions are paid to an HMRC-approved agency, and the funds are then distributed by the employee or under his or her instructions by the payroll giving agency.

Rent-a-room

Under the rent-a-room scheme, an individual taxpayer can receive up to £7500 a year tax-free from renting out a furnished room in a residential property. This reduces to £3750 if someone else receives income from letting accommodation in the same property, such as a joint owner. The limit is the same even if the accommodation is let for less than 12 months.

The scheme applies where a person lets furnished accommodation — a room or an entire floor of the home — to a lodger who pays to live in the home, sometimes with meals provided, and who occasionally shares the family rooms. In addition, the rent-a-room scheme can be used if the home is rented; the taxpayer does not have to be the owner-occupier.

CHAPTER 3

National Insurance

Class 1 Lower Earnings Limit

No National Insurance (NI) liability arises where earnings are below the lower earnings limit. Where earnings fall between the lower earnings limit and the earnings threshold, NI is payable at a notional zero rate. This preserves an employee's NI record and entitlement to certain contributory related benefits where earnings exceed the lower earnings limit.

The lower earnings limit also triggers entitlement to statutory maternity pay (SMP), statutory sick pay (SSP), statutory paternity pay (SPP), statutory adoption pay (SAP), statutory shared parental pay (ShPP) and to contributory benefits.

Class 1 Lower Earnings Limits

Tax year	Weekly	Monthly	Annual
2018/19	£116	£503	£6032
2017/18	£113	£490	£5876
2016/17	£112	£486	£5824
2015/16	£112	£486	£5824
2014/15	£111	£481	£5772
2013/14	£109	£473	£5668
2012/13	£107	£464	£5564
2011/12	£102	£442	£5304

Class 1 Earnings Thresholds

Employer's National Insurance Contributions (NICs) are payable if the employees' earnings reach or exceed the earnings threshold.

Employee's NICs are payable at the standard rate once the employee's earnings reach the earnings threshold.

Class 1 Earnings Thresholds

Tax year		Weekly	Monthly	Annual
2018/19	Joint	£162	£702	£8424
2017/18	Joint	£157	£680	£8164
2016/17	Employer's	£155	£672	£8060
	Employer's	£156	£676	£8112
2015/16	Employer's	£155	£672	£8060
	Employer's	£156	£676	£8112
2014/15	Employer's	£153	£663	£7956
	Employer's	£153	£663	£7956
2013/14	Employer's	£148	£641	£7696
	Employer's	£149	£646	£7755
2012/13	Employer's	£144	£624	£7488
	Employer's	£146	£633	£7605
2011/12	Employer's	£136	£589	£7072
	Employer's	£139	£602	£7225

If the earnings period is a number of days, weeks or months rather than one week or one month, the earnings threshold must be calculated by dividing the annual figure by 365, 52 or 12, and multiplying the number of days, weeks or months as appropriate.

Class 1 Upper Earnings Limit

An employee whose weekly or monthly earnings exceed the upper earnings limit pays NI at the main rate on earnings above the earnings threshold up to that limit. The annual limit applies to directors. Employees pay NI at the additional 2% rate on earnings in excess of the upper earnings limit.

Rates for Class 1 Upper Earnings Limit

Tax year	Weekly	Monthly	Annual
2018/19	£892	£3863	£46,350
2017/18	£866	£3750	£45,000
2016/17	£827	£3583	£43,000
2015/16	£815	£3532	£42,385
2014/15	£805	£3489	£41,865
2013/14	£797	£3454	£41,450
2012/13	£817	£3540	£42,475
2011/12	£817	£3540	£42,475

Employer's Class 1 Rates for Employees

Employers pay secondary Class 1 NICs at the secondary rate on all earnings above the earnings threshold.

Secondary (Employers') Class 1 Rate

Tax year	Secondary rate
2011/12–2018/19	13.8%
2010/11	12.8%

Employee's Class 1 Rates for Employees

From 2003/04, the employee pays NICs on earnings in excess of the upper earnings limit, but at the additional percentage rate.

Employee's Class 1 Rates for Employees

Year	Standard rate (%)	Reduced rate (%)	Additional rate (%)
2011/12–2018/19	12.00	5.85	2.00
2008/09–2010/11	11.00	4.85	1.00

Class 1 Contracted-out Rates

If an employee is a member of an approved contracted-out employer's pension scheme, he or she was contracted out of S2P. Both the employer and employee paid a reduced rate of NI between the lower and upper earnings limits only. There was no reduction in the NI rates for income above the upper earnings limit for employers or (for 2003/04 onwards) for employees. For 1999/2000 onwards, this meant that the employer was entitled to a rebate on earnings between the lower earnings limit and the employer's earnings threshold. For 2000/01 onwards an employee's rebate was due on earnings between the lower earnings limit and the employee's earnings threshold. If the rebate exceeded the employee's contributions the excess could be retained by the employer and not paid to the employee.

The contracted-out reduction differed between contracted-out salary related (COSR) schemes and contracted-out money purchase (COMP) schemes. It is not available for COMP schemes for 2012/13 onwards and for COSR schemes for 2016/17 onwards due to the introduction of a flat-rate State pension. For COSR schemes, the reduction was given through a contracted-out rebate of a fixed percentage, irrespective of age. For COMP schemes, the reduction was age-related and was given partly by means of a contracted-out rebate of a fixed percentage, with the age-related element being paid by the HMRC NICs Office to the COMP scheme at the end of the year. The rebates are given in the table below.

Contracting-out Rebates

Years	Employer's reduction (%)	Employee's reduction (%)
2012/13 to 2015/16	3.4 (COSR) n/a (COMP)	1.4
2007/08 to 2011/12	3.7 (COSR) 1.4 (COMP)	1.6

Class 1A Rates

Class 1A NICs are payable on the cash equivalent of benefits in kind provided to P11D employees and directors.

Class 1A NICs are paid by the employer only. They must be paid by 19 July (or 22 July, if paid electronically) after the tax year of assessment. The rates are as follows.

Class 1A Rates

Tax year	Rate (%)
2011/12–2018/19	13.8
2008/09–2010/11	12.8

Class 1B Rates

Class 1B NI is payable, by employers only, on items covered by a PAYE settlement agreement (including the grossed-up tax). It is payable if the item would otherwise have been liable to Class 1 or 1A NICs.

Class 1B Rates

Tax year	Rate (%)
2011/12–2018/19	13.8
2007/08–2010/11	12.8

Class 2, 3 and 4 Rates

Class 2 NI is paid by the self-employed at a fixed weekly amount, unless their income from self-employment is less than the small profits exemption limit. There are special rates for share fishermen and certain voluntary workers. Class 2 NI will be abolished from April 2019.

Class 3 is a voluntary contribution which may be paid by anyone whose NI record would otherwise be insufficient for them to qualify for contributory social security benefits.

Class 4 is paid by the self-employed as a percentage of their profits between a lower and upper annual limit. Class 4 contributions are paid at the additional 2% rate on profits in excess of the upper limit.

Class 2, 3 and 4 Rates

	Class 2		Class 3		Class 4		
Tax year	Weekly amount	Small earnings exemption	Weekly amount	Lower annual limit	Upper annual limit	Main rate (%)	Add'l rate (%)
2018/19	£2.95	£6205	£14.65	£8424	£46,350	9.0	2.0
2017/18	£2.85	£6025	£14.25	£8164	£45,000	9.0	2.0
2016/17	£2.80	£5965	£13.80	£8060	£43,000	9.0	2.0
2015/16	£2.80	£5965	£13.80	£8060	£42,385	9.0	2.0
2014/15	£2.75	£5885	£13.90	£7956	£41,865	9.0	2.0
2013/14	£2.70	£5725	£13.55	£7755	£41,450	9.0	2.0
2012/13	£2.65	£5595	£13.25	£7605	£42,475	9.0	2.0
2011/12	£2.50	£5315	£12.60	£7225	£42,475	9.0	2.0

Annual Maxima

There is no annual maximum liability for secondary contributions.

However, there is an annual maximum contribution liability for an employed earner or a self-employed earner.

Following the introduction of the additional primary rate on earnings above the upper earnings limit, the annual maxima is computed in accordance with a complex formula.

Employees' Own Cars — Mileage Allowance

Most employers reimburse employees who use their own cars on company business. The reimbursement is usually by way of a mileage allowance. There is no liability for NI provided the allowance paid does not exceed specified maximum amounts. If it does, the excess is liable to NI through the payroll.

National Insurance Rates for 2002/03 onwards

From 6 April 2002, the specified maximum mileage rate for cars is the HMRC authorised mileage rate for 10,000 business miles, regardless of the total number of business miles travelled during the tax year. The rate is given on page 25.

HMRC authorised mileage rates are also used for bicycles (from 6 April 1999) and motorbikes (from 6 April 2000) — see page 25.

CHAPTER 4

Pensions Data

Overview of System

A pension can currently come from four main sources.
1. State schemes.
2. Occupational pension schemes.
3. Personal pension schemes.
4. Stakeholder pension schemes.

State Schemes

A State pension is payable on reaching State pension age to a person whose contribution record is sufficient. Since its introduction, the State pension has undergone various reforms. A two-tier State pension comprising the basic State pension and the earnings-related second State pension is payable to qualifying individuals who reached State pension age on or before 5 April 2016. Qualifying individuals who reach State pension age on or after 6 April 2016 receive the new single-tier State pension.

To cope with an ageing population, the pension age is being increased. The pension age for women is being gradually increased from 60 to 65 between 2010 and 2018. Once the State pension age has been equalised for men and women, it is to be further increased. It will reach 66 for both men and women on 6 October 2020.

Men who were born before 6 December 1953 reach State pension age on their 65th birthday.

The **Pensions Act 1995** provides that women born after 5 April 1950 but before 6 December 1953 have a State pension age of between 60 and 65 depending on their date of birth, as shown in the table below.

Women's State Pension Age under the Pensions Act 1995

Date of birth	Date State pension age reached
6 April 1950–5 May 1950	6 May 2010
6 May 1950–5 June 1950	6 July 2010
6 June 1950–5 July 1950	6 September 2010
6 July 1950–5 August 1950	6 November 2010
6 August 1950–5 September 1950	6 January 2011
6 September 1950–5 October 1950	6 March 2011
6 October 1950–5 November 1950	6 May 2011
6 November 1950–5 December 1950	6 July 2011
6 December 1950–5 January 1951	6 September 2011
6 January 1951–5 February 1951	6 November 2011
6 February 1951–5 March 1951	6 January 2012
6 March 1951–5 April 1951	6 March 2012
6 April 1951–5 May 1951	6 May 2012
6 May 1951–5 June 1951	6 July 2012
6 June 1951–5 July 1951	6 September 2012
6 July 1951–5 August 1951	6 November 2012
6 August 1951–5 September 1951	6 January 2013
6 September 1951–5 October 1951	6 March 2013
6 October 1951–5 November 1951	6 May 2013
6 November 1951–5 December 1951	6 July 2013
6 December 1951–5 January 1952	6 September 2013
6 January 1952–5 February 1952	6 November 2013
6 February 1952–5 March 1952	6 January 2014
6 March 1952–5 April 1952	6 March 2014
6 April 1952–5 May 1952	6 May 2014
6 May 1952–5 June 1952	6 July 2014
6 June 1952–5 July 1952	6 September 2014

Date of birth	Date State pension age reached
6 July 1952–5 August 1952	6 November 2014
6 August 1952–5 September 1952	6 January 2015
6 September 1952–5 October 1952	6 March 2015
6 October 1952–5 November 1952	6 May 2015
6 November 1952–5 December 1952	6 July 2015
6 December 1952–5 January 1953	6 September 2015
6 January 1953–5 February 1953	6 November 2015
6 February 1953–5 March 1953	6 January 2016
6 March 1953–5 April 1953	6 March 2016

Increase to State pension age
Provisions introduced by the **Pensions Act 2011** (amending schedule 4 to the **Pensions Act 1995**) increase the State pension age for women to 65 between April 2016 and November 2018. From December 2018, the State pension age for both men and women is to start to increase to reach age 66 in October 2020.

These changes affect a:
- woman born on or after 6 April 1953
- man born on or after 6 December 1953.

The following two tables show when individuals will reach the new State pension age and the age at which they will do so.

Changes to State Pension Equalisation Timetable for Women

Period within which birthday falls	Date new State pension age reached	New State pension age in years and months
6 April 1953–5 May 1953	6 July 2016	63 years 2 months–63 years 3 months
6 May 1953–5 June 1953	6 November 2016	63 years 5 months–63 years 6 months
6 June 1953–5 July 1953	6 March 2017	63 years 8 months–63 years 9 months
6 July 1953–5 August 1953	6 July 2017	63 years 11 months–63 years 0 month

Period within which birthday falls	Date new State pension age reached	New State pension age in years and months
6 August 1953–5 September 1953	6 November 2017	64 years 2 months–64 years 3 months
6 September 1953–5 October 1953	6 March 2018	64 years 5 months–64 years 6 months
6 October 1953–5 November 1953	6 July 2018	64 years 8 months–64 years 9 months
6 November 1953–5 December 1953	6 November 2018	64 years 11 months–65 years

Increase in State Pension Age from 65 to 66 for Men and Women

Date of birth	Date State pension age reached
6 December 1953–5 January 1954	6 March 2019
6 January 1954–5 February 1954	6 May 2019
6 February 1954–5 March 1954	6 July 2019
6 March 1954–5 April 1954	6 September 2019
6 April 1954–5 May 1954	6 November 2019
6 May 1954–5 June 1954	6 January 2020
6 June 1954–5 July 1954	6 March 2020
6 July 1954–5 August 1954	6 May 2020
6 August 1954–5 September 1954	6 July 2020
6 September 1954–5 October 1954	6 September 2020
6 October 1954–5 April 1960	66th birthday

Further provisions contained in the **Pensions Act 2014** (further amending schedule 4 to the **Pensions Act 1995**) brought forward the increase in the State pension age from 66 to 67 by eight years such that the State pension age for both men and women will rise from 66 to 67 between 2026 and 2028 depending on date of birth. This change affects men and women born after 5 April 1961 but before 6 April 1969 who will now have a State pension age of 67.

Men and women born after 5 April 1960 but before 6 April 1961 will reach State pension age between 66 and 67 as shown in the following table. The **Pensions Act 2007** provides for the State pension age to increase from 67 to 68 between 2046 and 2048. The impact of this increase, as the law currently stands, is shown in the table below. However, it was announced in July 2017 that following a review, the Government plans to bring forward the increase in the State pension age from 67 to 68 by nine years so that it would rise to 68 between 2037 and 2039 rather than between 2046 and 2048.

Increase in State Pension Age from 66 to 67 for Men and Women

Date of birth	Date State pension age reached
6 April 1960–5 May 1960	66 years and 1 month
6 May 1960–5 June 1960	66 years and 2 months
6 June 1960–5 July 1960	66 years and 3 months
6 July 1960–5 August 1960	66 years and 4 months[1]
6 August 1960–5 September 1960	66 years and 5 months
6 September 1960–5 October 1960	66 years and 6 months
6 October 1960–5 November 1960	66 years and 7 months
6 November 1960–5 December 1960	66 years and 8 months
6 December 1960–5 January 1961	66 years and 9 months[2]
6 January 1961–5 February 1961	66 years and 10 months[3]
6 February 1961–5 March 1961	66 years and 11 months
6 March 1961–5 April 1977*	67 years

*For people born after 5 April 1969 but before 6 April 1977, under the **Pensions Act 2007**, State pension age was already 67.
For the purposes of calculating an individual's State pension age, the following applies.
[1] A person born on 31 July 1960 is considered to reach the age of 66 years and 4 months on 30 November 2026.
[2] A person born on 31 December 1960 is considered to reach the age of 66 years and 9 months on 30 September 2027.
[3] A person born on 31 January 1961 is considered to reach the age of 66 years and 10 months on 30 November 2027.

Further changes to State pension age

Section 27 of the **Pensions Act 2014** introduced provisions to facilitate the periodic review of the State pension age. The legislation requires the Secretary of State to review the pensionable age from time to time having regard to life expectancy and other factors, and to prepare and publish a report on the outcome of the review. The first such review had to take place before May 2017 and each subsequent report must be published at intervals of six years or less.

Following the first review, the Government announced in July 2019 that the increase in the State pension age from 67 to 68 would be brought forward so as to take place between 2037 and 2039 rather than between 2047 and 2048 as currently legislated.

Basic State Pension — People Reaching State Pension Age on or Before 5 April 2016

Under the two-tier State pension that applies to people who reached State pension age before 6 April 2016, people who have paid sufficient qualifying contributions receive the basic State pension and may also receive the earnings-related second State pension. A person who reached State pension age on or after 6 April 2010 and before 6 April 2016 needed 30 qualifying years for the full basic State pension. The basic State pension for a single person is £122.30 per week for 2017/18, increasing to £125.95 per week for 2018/19. The amount that a married couple will receive depends on whether both partners have sufficient qualifying years for the basic State pension. If so they will receive £122.30 each for 2017/18 (£245 between them) and £125.95 each for 2018/19 (£251.90 between them). If one partner has not built up his or her own record and claims on his or her partner's record, that partner will receive up to £73.30 per week for 2017/18 (a total for the couple of £195.60) and £75.50 for 2018/19 (a total of £201.45).

People on low income can boost their income by claiming pension credit. This can increase income to £159.35 for a single person and to £243.55 for a couple for 2017/18, and to £163.00 for a single person and £248.80 for a couple for 2018/19. Additional amounts are payable to carers and to persons who are severely disabled.

Second State Pensions — People Reaching State Pension Age on or Before 6 April 2016

The two-tier State pension system applicable to those who reached State pension age on or before 5 April 2016 comprises the basic State pension and an earnings-related second pension. The Government has run three schemes to provide a second-tier pension on top of the basic State pension. Between April 1961 and April 1975, employees bought units of graduated pension. From 6 April 1978 to 5 April 2002, the State ran the State earnings-related pension scheme (SERPS), which was replaced, with effect from 6 April 2002, with another earnings-related plan called the State Second Pension (S2P). The two-tier State pension is replaced by a single-tier State pension for people who reach State pension age on or after 6 April 2016. An earnings-related second State pension will only be paid to eligible people who reached State pension age before 6 April 2016. However, those eligible to receive the second State pension will continue to receive it beyond April 2016.

Prior to 6 April 2012, it was possible to contract out of the second State pension and instead top-up the basic State pension by means of a personal or occupational pension. However, since 6 April 2012, it has not been possible to contract out using defined contribution (DC) (money purchase) arrangements. Consequently, contracting out for personal and stakeholder pensions, and money purchase occupational schemes came to an end on 5 April 2012.

Until 5 April 2016, it remained possible to contract out of S2P by means of a defined benefit (DB) (final salary) scheme. However, as a result of the introduction of the single-tier State pension and the abolition of the earnings-related second State pension for people reaching State pension age on or after 6 April 2016 contracting out for DB schemes came to an end on that date.

Since it is extraordinarily difficult for individuals to calculate their State pension entitlements, their easiest option is to use the Department for Work and Pensions (DWP) forecast service, triggered by obtaining Form BR19 from their local office or using the Pension Service's online form and following the instructions shown.

Single-tier State Pension

The single-tier State pension system applies to people who reach State pension age on or after 6 April 2016 and whose contributions record is sufficient. To qualify for the full single-tier State pension a person must have 35 qualifying years. People with less than 35 qualifying years will receive a reduced pension. However, the single-tier State pension will not be paid to persons with less than 10 qualifying years. Eligibility depends on the individual's own contributions record. Contributions paid by a spouse or civil partner will not be taken into account. The single-tier pension is set at £159.55 per week for 2017/18, rising to £164.35 for 2018/19. People who reached State pension age before 6 April 2016 will continue to receive the two-tier State pension rather than the new single-tier State pension beyond 6 April 2016.

Work-based Pensions

Work-based pensions provided by employers for the benefit of their employees can take the legal form of an *occupational pension scheme*, or of a *group personal pension (GPP) arrangement*, or of a *designated stakeholder pension scheme*, or an employer may agree to pay a contribution directly into the *personal pension* or *stakeholder pension scheme* that has been individually selected by an employee. Progressively, since 1 October 2012, employers have been required to enrol employees who are aged 22 and over, who earn more than the earnings trigger for automatic enrolment, set at £10,000 for both 2017/18 and 2018/19, and who work in the UK into an eligible workplace pension scheme. The date from which auto-enrolment applies (known as the staging date) depends on the number of employees that the employer has. As part of the introduction of auto-enrolment, a new national pensions savings scheme known as the National Employment Savings Trust (NEST) was introduced. Employers, however, who provide work-based pension schemes that meet the designated quality requirements may offer these schemes to their employees rather than NEST.

Occupational Schemes

With important exceptions (see *Transferred Employees* below), employers are not currently obliged to operate an occupational scheme, but if they do, the scheme must comply with stringent regulations.

Such a scheme is usually registered with HM Revenue & Customs (HMRC). This means that employees' contributions are fully tax-relieved, employers' contributions count as a business expense, and the scheme may generally earn income and capital gains tax-free.

Occupational pension schemes may be:
- defined benefit schemes
- defined contribution schemes
- cash balance schemes.

The term "defined benefit (DB) scheme" means that the pension payable is usually related to the member's salary. It is a *final salary scheme* if the pension is related to the member's earnings over a defined period shortly before the member begins to draw the pension or otherwise ceases to be an active member of the scheme (eg by ceasing to be an employee of that employer). It is an *average salary scheme* if the pension is related to the member's annual earnings during the entire period of that employee's active membership of the scheme. Under DC schemes (also known as money purchase schemes), the pension is usually based on immediate annuity rates and the amount of contributions attributable to the employee when he or she begins to draw the pension, taking account of the investment roll up, less any charges. The benefit is directly attributable to the value of assets and the scheme can therefore never fall into deficit. There is a further kind of occupational pension scheme known as a *cash balance scheme* in which a defined proportion of the employee's earnings is notionally added to the member's account each year, say 25% of earnings, but the amount of the pension itself will depend on the value of the annuity that the accumulated fund allocated to the member's account can secure. The member's rights to benefit accrue therefore on a DB basis but the actual pension secured by those rights is secured in the same way as in a DC scheme.

Personal and Stakeholder Pensions

Personal pension plans were introduced on 1 July 1988. Personal pensions are always based on the money purchase principle.

Prior to 6 April 2006 there were restrictions placed on employees pensioning the same earnings using both an occupational pension scheme and a personal pension scheme, but since that date there has been "full concurrency", meaning that an individual may simultaneously build up rights under one or more occupational and personal pension schemes. From 8 October 2001 until 30 September 2012, employers with at least five employees had to offer employees access to a stakeholder pension which the employer has designated (unless the employer provides an occupational pension scheme open to all employees or a GPP scheme meeting certain conditions). There was no requirement for the employer itself to contribute to a stakeholder pension scheme that it had designated. In practice, a stakeholder pension was almost invariably also legally established as a personal pension. The main differences between a personal pension and a stakeholder pension is that a stakeholder pension is subject to a cap on the charges that the pension provider can make and must provide a default investment fund to those members who do not wish to decide into which funds to invest.

The requirement for employers to provide access to a designated stakeholder pension was removed from 1 October 2012 as a consequence of the introduction of auto-enrolment.

An employer may agree to pay contributions directly into the personal pension or the stakeholder pension scheme that an individual employee has chosen, or has been invited to choose individually. Many more employees, however, are in membership of GPP arrangements or a stakeholder pension scheme which the employer has designated for use by its employees. If the employer also agrees to contribute to such group schemes, the employer may freely promote membership of that GPP arrangement or designated stakeholder pension without falling foul of the prohibition of promoting an investment product without authorisation under the financial services legislation. This is subject to the employer not benefiting, for example, from commission payments when it enrols employees into these schemes and notifying the employee of the amount of contribution that the employer will pay. With the introduction of automatic enrolment, obligation for an employer to provide access to a stakeholder pension or suitable alternative was withdrawn from 1 October 2012 subject to the employer continuing to provide a direct payment facility for those who enjoyed the facility on 1 October 2012 until they leave service.

Transferred Employees

Employers which have acquired part of a public sector enterprise, and the employees going with it, are obliged to offer an occupational scheme. Further, with effect from 6 April 2005, employees transferred from one private sector employer to another have to be offered pension rights if they were, or could have been, members of their original employer's work-based scheme.

Pensioners' Income Data

The Government publishes annual statistics on the levels and trends of pensioners' income based on a two-person household. The tables reproduced below relate to 2015/16 figures as published in March 2017 (see *www.gov.uk/government/statistics*). The table below shows the average incomes for State pensioner couples (currently defined as married or cohabiting couples where at least one party is over State pension age) and single pensioners (people over State pension age).

Average Pensioner Incomes 2015/16

	£ per week 2015/16 prices	Percentage of gross income
All pensioners		
Gross income from:		
Benefit income	218	43%
Occupational pension	149	29%
Personal pension	19	4%
Investment income	42	8%
Earnings	81	16%
Other income	4	1%
Total	512	100%
Pensioner couples		
Gross income from		
Benefit income	250	35%
Occupational pension	216	30%
Personal pension	29	4%
Investment income	68	10%
Earnings	144	20%
Other income	5	1%
Total	713	100%
Single pensioners		
Gross income from:		
Benefit income	188	57%
Occupational pension	26	26%
Personal pension	9	3%
Investment income	18	6%
Earnings	22	7%
Other income	3	1%
Total	327	100%
Source: DWP Pensioners' Incomes Series 2015/16 (updated March 2017)		

Pensioners have seen an increase in their average weekly incomes over the past decade. After the deduction of direct taxes and housing costs, the average income of all pensioners was £296 per week for 2015/16 compared to £258 per week for 2005/06.

Recently, retired pensioners (those where the head of the household was within five years of State pension age) and pensioners where the head of the household was under 75 had higher incomes than those where the head of the household was 75 or over. The difference was statistically significant. In 2005/06 and 2015/16, the income of pensioners, who were 75 or over, was 75% of that of those under 75. These statistics reflect the fact that younger pensioners are likely to be in work and have higher gross mean income from earnings — £134 per week where the head of the household is under 75. Further, younger pensioners are more likely to have benefited from the peak in occupational scheme savings in the late 1980s.

In 2015/16, the average income for pensioner couples was more than twice that of single pensioners. The income difference between pensioner couples and single pensioners has increased over the past decade. In 2005/06 pensioner couples' average (median) income was £183 more than the average (median) single pensioner income; in 2015/16 it was £231 more. Pensioner couples are more likely to be in receipt of private pension income than single pensioners (81% compared to 61%). For pensioners with a source of private pension income, pensioner couples received double the amount of single pensioners (£206 compared to £103). Pensioner couples were also more likely to be in receipt of earnings than single pensioners (27% compared to 7%), although this may reflect that in a pensioner couple, one partner is under pension age and still working (61% of pensioner couples where one partner was under State pension age had earnings compared to 17% of pensioner couples where both were over State pension age).

There was also a gender difference in pensioner income. Single male pensioners had higher average incomes than single female pensioners; a difference that was greatest in those aged under 75. Single men in this age group had an average income of £224 per week compared to single female pensioners in this age group who had an average income of £203 per week. The difference reflects higher occupational income among single men; £104 per week compared to £78 per week for single women. However, women have participated in occupational pensions more in recent decades. On average, single male pensioners had higher personal pension income than single female pensioners.

Pensioner incomes also showed regional variations. Pensioner couple incomes were the lowest in Wales and the West Midlands, and highest in the South East.

Single pensioners in Wales and the North East had the lowest income, while those in Scotland and the South East had the highest.

State Retirement Pension

State retirement pension is the main State benefit payable to pensioners. The nature of the State retirement pension that is received depends on the date on which the pensioner reaches State pension age. Where a person reached State pension age on or before 5 April 2016, the State pension comprises two separate components — the basic State pension and additional pension from either the SERPS which ran from 1978 to 2002 or the S2P which began in 2002.

The average weekly amount of State retirement pension in payment, basic State pension and additional pension from SERPS/S2P combined, to those who have reached State pension age for recent times is shown in the table below. The table shows the average weekly amount of State retirement pension payable to all those in receipt.

Mean Income from State Pensioners £ per week (2015/16 prices)

	All pensioner units	Pension couples	Single pensioners
1994/95	116	143	98
1995/96	114	139	96
1996/97	119	145	100
1997/98	120	149	100
1998/99	122	150	102
1999/00	126	155	106
2000/01	128	156	107
2001/02	137	167	114
2002/03	141	171	116
2003/04	143	174	118
2004/05	146	177	120
2005/06	151	181	126

	All pensioner units	Pension couples	Single pensioners
2006/07	152	182	127
2007/08	155	186	128
2008/09	158	186	132
2009/10	167	198	137
2010/11	165	195	137
2011/12	165	195	134
2012/13	171	207	138
2013/14	171	209	136
2014/15	175	215	137
2015/16	179	220	140

Source: *Pensioners' Incomes Series: An Analysis of Trends in Pensioner Incomes: 1994/95 to 2015/16.*

Pension Credit

Under the two-tier State pension scheme that applies to pensioners who reached State pension age on or before 5 April 2016, the second most important State benefit payable to pensioners is the State pension credit, which is a means-tested benefit, and which comprises two separate components — the *guarantee credit* and the *savings credit*.

Before 6 April 2010, the guarantee credit was payable to an eligible single pensioner aged 60 or over, or to an eligible pensioner couple where one of the partners was aged 60 or over. From 6 April 2010, however, the age at which an eligible single pensioner or an eligible pensioner couple can receive guarantee credit is increasing in line with the increase in the State pension age applicable to women. The standard minimum guarantee was set at £155.60 for a single person and £237.55 for a couple for 2016/17; and increased to £159.35 for a single person and £243.25 for a couple for 2017/18, increasing to £163 for a single person and £248.80 for a couple for 2018/19. The single-tier State pension, which was introduced for people reaching State pension age on or after 6 April 2016, is set at a level that is at least equal to the standard minimum guarantee. For 2017/18, the single-tier State pension was set at £159.55 per week, increasing to £164.35 per week for 2018/19.

From 2012/13 those over State pension age who have made some extra provision towards their retirement, such as savings or an occupational pension, may be entitled to receive savings credit if their income is more than the savings credit threshold.

For 2017/18 the savings credit thresholds were £137.35 for a single person and £218.42 for a couple. They are increased to £140.67 for a single person and £223.82 for a couple for 2018/19.

The maximum amount payable through savings credit was set at £13.20 for a single person and at £14.90 for a couple for 2017/18, and at £13.40 for a single person and £14.99 for a couple for 2018/19.

Prevalence of Work-based Pensions

Prior to an employer being brought within auto-enrolment (and subject to meeting the access requirements for stakeholder pensions that applied prior to 1 October 2012) there was no requirement for an employer to provide a workplace pension and the provision of such a pension was voluntary. However, the introduction of auto-enrolment which is being introduced progressively from October 2012, will mean that once an employer reaches its staging date, that employer will be required to enrol eligible employers in an eligible workplace pension and to meet certain minimum contribution standards. Employees do, however, have the option to opt out of auto-enrolment.

Prior to auto-enrolment, whether or not a private sector employer made private work-based provision for its employees was strongly correlated to the size of the employer as measured by the number of its employees. The overall extent of provision at that time is shown below.

Overall Incidence and Type of Provision among Organisations, by Size of Organisation

Number of employees									
Type of pension provision	1–4	5–9	10–19	20–49	50–99	100–499	500–999	1000+	All
Any occupational scheme	1%	4%	11%	8%	15%	28%	48%	74%	3%
Defined benefit	0%	2%	4%	4%	7%	21%	39%	50%	1%
Defined contribution	1%	1%	3%	2%	7%	8%	13%	24%	1%
Hybrid	0%	0%	1%	1%	1%	1%	5%	10%	0%
GPP scheme	2%	6%	9%	17%	32%	46%	52%	50%	5%

Number of employees									
Type of pension provision	1–4	5–9	10–19	20–49	50–99	100–499	500–999	1000+	All
GSIPP	1%	1%	2%	0%	2%	2%	8%	5%	1%
Workplace-based SHP scheme	10%	33%	53%	59%	57%	54%	48%	55%	19%
Contributions to personal pensions	9%	7%	15%	18%	14%	23%	24%	16%	10%
Any pension provisions	21%	42%	69%	76%	83%	92%	99%	100%	31%
Any workplace pension scheme	13%	39%	65%	71%	82%	90%	98%	99%	24%

Source: Table 2.3 Employers' Pension Provision Survey 2011, DWP Research Report No. 802. John Forth, Lucy Stokes, Alice Fitzpatrick and Catherine Grant.

Note: The figures for "any pension provisions" may be lower than the sum of the individual forms of provision since some firms may provide more than one type of scheme.

"Any workplace pension scheme" refers to the provision of an occupational scheme, a GPP scheme or a workplace-based SHP scheme. It excludes contributions to either personal pensions or private SHPs.

Defined Benefit Occupational Pension Schemes

Data on those DB occupational pension schemes that are liable to pay the scheme-based and risk-based pension protection levies are reported in the Pensions Regulator's *Purple Book*, which is published annually. The main body of the analysis in the Purple Book, which is published annually. The data contained in the 2017 edition (which is available to download from the pension protection fund website at *www.pensionprotectionfund.org.uk*), is based on schemes return for a dataset of 5588 DB schemes issued in December 2016 and January 2017 and returned to the regulator by the end of March 2017. The data covers 10.5 million memberships. This represents virtually all Pension Protection Fund (PPF) eligible schemes and universe liabilities. The eligible universe of schemes was estimated at 5671, down from 5886 in March 2016.

Note: *Section 179 liabilities are the liabilities of a DB occupational pension scheme which are eligible to cover from the PPF, as calculated in an actuarial valuation carried out under s.179 of the **Pensions Act 2004** to determine for the purpose of calculating the risk-based levy.

The *Purple Book* focuses on the risk to scheme members of not receiving promised benefits and of claims on the PPF. These risks, in turn, depend on two key elements: the risk of the sponsoring employer becoming insolvent and the extent of scheme underfunding.

Defined Contribution (DC) Provision

Employer provided pension schemes can take the following forms.

1. A trust-based DC occupational pension scheme which has been established by the employer or a group of employers and which is primarily regulated by the Pensions Regulator.
2. A contract-based arrangement whereby the employer has entered into an arrangement with a provider of either a personal pension scheme or stakeholder pension scheme whereby the employer will enter into a direct payment arrangement with that provider to forward both the employer's contributions and those from the employee. Contract-based schemes are primarily regulated by the Financial Services Authority.
3. Where an employer agrees to make a direct contribution to a contract-based personal or stakeholder pension which has individually been chosen by an employee.

The Pensions Regulator's ninth edition of its annual statistics on DC trust-based pension schemes and members (2017/18), published in January 2018, reported the following pension data based on a wide-ranging data set of 32,720 occupational schemes with two or more DC members (including hybrids, of which 30,530 (93%) are micro schemes).

Defined Benefit Schemes

There were 5794 DB schemes, of which 737 (13%) were still open schemes. The total number of memberships was 10.9 million.

Hybrid Mixed Benefit Schemes

There were 180 hybrid mixed benefit schemes, of which 20 were still open schemes.

The total number of memberships was 621,000 and the total number of active members was 55,000.

Hybrid Dual Section

There were 910 hybrid-dual section schemes, of which 440 were still open schemes.

The total number of memberships was 5.370 million and the total number of active members was 1.203 million.

DC Trust

There were 33,650 DC Trust schemes of which 26,240 were still open schemes.

The total number of memberships was 8.489 million and the total number of active members was 5.151 million.

DC Contract

The total number of DC contract arrangements was 2620 of which 2400 were still open. Total memberships were unknown. Total active memberships was estimated at 4.88 million.

The key findings reported by the Pensions Regulator were as follows.

1. There are around 34,500 schemes with DC trust-based members, of which 32,000 are micro schemes.
2. DC scheme volumes are stabilising, with a reduction of just 3% in the past year, though the number of schemes with 12-plus members has declined by 10%.
3. In 2009, only 66% of schemes had members aged over 50, this is now 98%, and represents around 20% of its members, consistent since 2009.
4. There are 87 master trusts with DC members registered [with the Pensions Regulator].
5. Less than half the schemes offer a default investment strategy, though more than two-thirds of open schemes do this.
6. Membership has increased by 42% since last year, and by over 300% since 2009.
7. 55% of all private sector workplace pension members are in DC schemes, and 86% of all those currently saving are investing into a DC scheme.
8. 92% of members are invested in the scheme's default strategy.
9. Assets increased by 17% this year, compared to 24% last year. The asset increase is made up of contributions (including transfers in) and investment returns, and is reduced by retirements and transfers out.
10. Asset values have increased by 23% last year, compared to 28% the year before.

11. Average assets per membership are £4700, a reduction from last year. This is driven by the huge influx of new memberships who started with no assets.
12. 750 schemes are being used for AE, up from 490 last year. Almost half of these schemes have fewer than 12 members.
13. 95% of members are in schemes being used for AE.
14. 72% of micro schemes are schemes formerly known as small self-administered schemes (SSASs). Relevant small schemes include schemes formerly known as SSAS and also executive pension plans. [The Pension Regulator] does not currently have a full cycle of date for whether micro schemes are EPPs.

Contracted-out Schemes

Contracting out was abolished from 6 April 2016 although guaranteed minimum pensions (pre-1997 accrual) will be retained.

COSR Schemes

Contracting out for contracted-out salary-related (COSR) schemes came to an end on 5 April 2016. From 6 April 1997 COSR schemes could only be contracted out if the "reference scheme test" was satisfied in exchange for flat percentage NIC rebates for employees and employers. The member ceased over the period from 6 April 1997 to 5 April 2002 to build up any further rights to additional pension from SERPS while in contracted-out employment (being contracted out under S2P instead). The scheme must provide benefits at least as good as those specified. These include:

- retirement at age 65
- a pension of at least $1/80^{th}$ of average qualifying earnings per year of service (maximum 40), where average qualifying earnings are 90% of earnings between the lower earnings limit (LEL) and the upper earnings limit (UEL) until 6 April 2009 when the UEL for this purpose was replaced by the Upper Accrual Point (UAP)
- a spouse's/civil partner's pension of at least 50% of the member's pension
- an annual increase of the lesser of 2.5% and the increase in the Retail Prices Index in relation to service from 6 April 2005, and the lower of 5% and the index in relation to periods of service from 6 April 1997 to 5 April 2005, but in recent years the Consumer Prices Index is used instead of the Retail Prices Index.

The scheme, contracted out or not, must meet the scheme funding requirements set out in Part 3 of the **Pensions Act 2004** and is subject to actuarial valuations.

For employment periods before 6 April 1997, a COSR scheme had to provide a guaranteed minimum pension (GMP) approximating to the additional pension from SERPS, and a "contracted-out deduction" was made from the SERPS pension that would otherwise have been paid.

When SERPS was replaced by S2P in April 2002 contracting-out arrangements continued much as before except that members who, if not contracted out, would have earned more S2P pension than in SERPS received a top-up amount through the State system.

Contracting out for COSR schemes came to an end on 5 April 2016. From 6 April 2016, it is no longer possible to build up entitlement to S2P as people who reach State pension age on or after 6 April 2016 fall within the single-tier pension scheme.

Contracted-out Money Purchase (COMP) Schemes

This method of contracting out using the protected rights test was abolished from 6 April 2012, as were protected rights.

Appropriate Personal Pensions

As in relation to contracted-out money purchase (COMP) schemes, Appropriate Personal Pension schemes ceased to be able to contract out employees for future service from 6 April 2012.

Registered Pension Schemes

The tax rules for registered pension schemes are contained in the **Finance Act 2004**. The main features of the pensions tax regime which have applied since 6 April 2006 are as follows.

- Tax relief on contributions is limited to the higher of £3600 a year and 100% of earnings.
- Tax-free retirement cash (now known as a "pension commencement lump sum") is limited to 25% of pension value, although when provided by a DB occupational pension scheme the pension value is 25% of the sum of the pension commencement lump sum itself and 20 times the annual value of the pension that is coming into payment.
- The amount of pension value added in a particular year will, if exceeding the available annual allowance be subject to an annual allowance charge. From 6 April 2011 this charge has been at a marginal

income tax rate (45% for 2015/16 and 2016/17) and will be met by the scheme member under self-assessment, although there will be an option to spread the charge or for the tax charge to be met from the individual's pension fund. Unused annual allowance from up to the three previous years in which the individual was a member of a registered pension scheme can offset pension savings in excess of the annual allowance.

The annual allowance is set at £40,000 for 2016/17, 2017/18 and 2018/19. However, where an individual has both threshold income in excess of £110,000 and adjusted net income in excess of £150,000, the annual allowance is reduced by £1 for every £2 by which adjusted net income exceeds £150,000, subject to a maximum reduction of £30,000. Consequently, where the abatement applies, anyone with an adjusted net income of £210,000 or more for 2016/17 and later tax years will receive only the minimum annual allowance of £10,000. However, as a result of alignment of the pension input period with the tax year from 6 April 2016, it was possible to have an annual allowance of £80,000 for 2015/16.

The 2015/16 tax year was split in two — the period from 5 April 2015 to 8 July 2015 (known as the "pre-alignment year") and the period from 9 July 2015 to 5 April 2016 (the post-alignment year). The annual allowance was set at £80,000 for the pre-alignment, but only £40,000 could be carried forward to the post-alignment year. To the extent that the annual allowance is unused it can be carried forward for up to three years. The annual allowance for the current year is used before any allowance brought forward, and allowances brought forward from an earlier year are used before those of a later year.

The second control on tax-relieved pension savings is the lifetime allowance, which places a limit on the pension pot. Where tax-relieved pension savings exceed the lifetime allowance, a tax charge (the lifetime allowance charge) is levied on the excess. The lifetime allowance was reduced from £1.25 million to £1 million from 6 April 2016, previously from £1.5 million to £1.25 million from 6 April 2014 and from £1.8 million to £1.5 million from 6 April 2012. Pension protection (individual protection) was available on the occasion of each reduction in the lifetime allowance to protect those whose pension savings were within the former lifetime allowance but exceeded the new reduced lifetime allowance.

The lifetime allowance has been set in the table below.

Lifetime Allowances

Tax year	Lifetime allowance
From 2016/17	£1,000,000
2014/15 and 2015/16	£1,250,000
2013/14	£1,500,000
2012/13	£1,500,000
2010/11 and 2011/12	£1,800,000

Annuity Rates

The table shows the standard annuity rates as at 17 January 2018 for a pension fund of £100,000 after the tax-free lump sum of £33,333 has been taken from a full fund of £133,333 for a single and joint relief basis. The tables have been taken from the Sharing Pensions website (see *www.sharingpensions.co.uk/annuity_rates.htm*).

Annuity Rates at Age 65

Single Standard Basis

Age	Level rate no guarantee	Level rate + 10-year guarantee	3% escalation no guarantee
55	£4158	£4135	£2625
60	£4680	£4645	£3009
65	£5476	£5394	£3787
70	£6075	£5915	£4412
75	£7105	£6744	£5351

Joint Standard Basis

Age	Level rate + 50% joint life	Level rate + 100% joint life	3% escalation + 50% joint life
55	3928	£3078	£2392
60	£4328	£4049	£2748

Joint Standard Basis

Age	Level rate + 50% joint life	Level rate + 100% joint life	3% escalation + 50% joint life
65	£5002	£4618	£3353
70	£5422	£5101	£3832
75	£5399	£5897	£4800

Note: Annuity rates based on a central London postcode (other locations such as Peterborough or Liverpool could be up to 4% higher or Dundee and Newcastle could be 5% higher) using a purchase price of £100,000 — this assumes an original pension fund of £133,333 and after the tax-free lump sum of £33,333 has been taken. Income is gross per year (before deduction of tax) and payable monthly in advance for the whole of the annuitant's life. No medical enhancements are included in these annuities. The pension annuity table is only a guide as annuities change frequently. Figures shown have been adjusted for Unisex annuity rates on a gender neutral basis and joint life rates assume both are the same age.

Life Expectancy Tables

The table is sourced from the Office for National Statistics (ONS) and shows the average number of years that people will live beyond their current age measured by "period life expectancy" analysed by age and sex for 2013–2015.

A life expectancy calculator based on current age and gender is available on the Office for National Statistics website (*https://visual.ons. gov.uk/what-is-my-life-expectancy-and-how-might-it-change*).

Life Expectancy Tables

Current age	Life expectancy (years)	
	Male	Female
0	79.09	82.82
1	78.43	82.11
2	77.46	81.13
3	76.47	80.14
4	75.48	79.15
5	74.49	78.16
6	73.50	77.16

	Life expectancy (years)	
Current age	Male	Female
7	72.50	76.17
8	71.51	75.17
9	70.51	74.18
10	69.52	73.18
11	68.53	72.19
12	67.53	71.19
13	66.54	70.20
14	65.55	69.20
15	64.56	68.21
16	63.57	67.22
17	62.58	66.23
18	61.60	65.24
19	60.62	64.26
20	59.65	63.27
21	58.68	62.28
22	57.71	61.29
23	56.73	60.31
24	55.76	59.32
25	54.79	58.33
26	53.83	57.35
27	52.86	56.36
28	51.89	55.38
29	50.92	54.40
30	49.96	53.41
31	49.00	52.43
32	48.03	51.46
33	47.07	50.48
34	46.11	49.50

Current age	Life expectancy (years)	
	Male	Female
35	45.16	48.53
36	44.20	47.56
37	43.25	46.59
38	42.30	45.62
39	41.36	44.65
40	40.42	43.69
41	39.48	42.73
42	38.54	41.77
43	37.61	40.81
44	36.68	39.86
45	35.75	38.91
46	34.83	37.96
47	33.92	37.02
48	33.00	36.08
49	32.09	35.14
50	31.18	34.21
51	30.28	33.28
52	29.39	32.35
53	28.49	31.44
54	27.61	30.52
55	26.73	29.61
56	25.86	28.71
57	24.99	27.81
58	24.14	26.92
59	23.30	26.04
60	22.47	25.16
61	21.64	24.29
62	20.83	23.42

Current age	Life expectancy (years)	
	Male	Female
63	20.03	22.57
64	19.23	21.72
65	18.45	20.87
66	17.68	20.04
67	16.90	19.20
68	16.14	18.38
69	15.39	17.58
70	14.66	16.78
71	13.95	15.99
72	13.24	15.22
73	12.57	14.46
74	11.90	13.72
75	11.26	12.99
76	10.62	12.28
77	10.01	11.58
78	9.40	10.90
79	8.82	10.23
80	8.25	9.59
81	7.72	8.97
82	7.20	8.38
83	6.71	7.81
84	6.25	7.27
85	5.81	6.76
86	5.40	6.27
87	5.01	5.81
88	4.65	5.38
89	4.32	4.98
90	4.00	4.60

	Life expectancy (years)	
Current age	Male	Female
91	3.71	4.26
92	3.43	3.94
93	3.19	3.64
94	2.98	3.39
95	2.78	3.15
96	2.59	2.93
97	2.40	2.71
98	2.24	2.52
99	2.12	2.36
100	1.99	2.22

Source: Office for National Statistics

Life Expectancy at Birth (England) and at Age 65

	Birth Male	Birth Female	Age 65 Male	Age 65 Female
UK 2014–2016	79.2	82.9	18.5	20.9

Source: National life tables, UK 2014 to 2016 (released 27 September 2017)

Lump Sum Commutation Factors

Members of occupational pension and personal or stakeholder pension schemes may take out a tax-free pension commencement lump sum on drawing a work-based pension. In the case of a DB occupational pension scheme, taking a lump sum reduces the amount of pension payable through a process called "commutation".

The rate at which commutation is given often depends on the:
• person's sex
• person's age
• rate of pension increase offered on the pension.

The table below gives historic commutation rates for males and females for any specified age but where no account has been taken of the rate of pension increase.

It shows the lump sum payable for each £1 forgone as annual pension. It should be adjusted by adding 0.02 for each month since the last birthday.

In practice, commutation rates which do take some account of pension increases lie mainly between £10 and £12 for men at 65, and between £12 and £14 for women at 60. There is no general legal requirement to equalise commutation rates between the sexes.

Historic Commutation Rates

Age	Male	Female
55	11.40	12.20
56	11.16	11.96
57	10.92	11.72
58	10.68	11.48
59	10.44	11.24
60	10.20	11.00
61	9.96	10.76
62	9.72	10.52
63	9.48	10.28
64	9.24	10.04
65	9.00	9.80
66	8.76	9.56
67	8.52	9.32
68	8.28	9.08
69	8.04	8.84
70	7.80	8.60
Source: HMRC		

Contributions to Defined Contribution Schemes

HMRC publishes personal pension statistics, which are available on the GOV.UK website (*www.gov.uk/government/statistics/personal-pensions-statistics-introduction*). At the time of writing, the figures were last updated on 29 September 2017. The figures show that in 2015/16, £24.3 billion was contributed to personal pensions. The proportion of payments contributed by employers increased to 59% from 54% in 2014/15. The number of individuals contributing to a personal pension increased to 9 million in 2015/16. This is the highest level since the statistics began and an increase on the 7.9 million people contributing in 2014/15. With auto-enrolment, this is likely to increase further. Average contributions increased to £2690 in 2015/16, up from £2540 in 2014/15.

Self-administered Pension Funds

A self-administered pension fund is an occupational pension scheme that is not a scheme where the sole long-term investment medium is an insurance policy.

Income and Expenditure of Self-administered Pension Funds

The quarterly business monitor MQ5, published by the ONS, contains income and expenditure data for self-administered pension schemes. The monitor can be downloaded from the ONS website (*www.ons.gov.uk*).

Employer-sponsored Stakeholder Pension Schemes

HMRC publishes stakeholder pension statistics, which are available on the GOV.UK website (see *www.gov.uk/government/statistics/stakeholder-pensions-for-individuals-annual-contributions*). At the time of writing the latest update was February 2017. The figures show that in 2015/16 individual contributions to stakeholder pension schemes totalled £1270 million and employer contributions totalled £2000 million (giving total contribution of £3270 million). From 1 October 2012 employers are no longer required to designate a stakeholder pension or suitable alternative, although existing direct payment arrangements (collection of contributions through payroll) must be continued.

Auto-enrolment

From October 2012 there is a requirement on employers to automatically enrol all their *eligible jobholders* into a *qualifying scheme*. An individual who is automatically enrolled by his or her employer remains free to opt out at any time, but must take action to do so.

If the jobholder has opted out, the employer must automatically re-enrol that eligible jobholder if he or she is still a jobholder of the employer. The re-enrolment process occurs about every three years. The employer's staging date is set by law and is based on the number of employees in the Pay As You Earn (PAYE) scheme on 1 April 2012. If the number of persons in the PAYE scheme changes after this date, the staging date is unaffected.

The table below sets out the revised automatic enrolment dates for all employer sizes.

Staging Dates by PAYE Scheme Size or Reference

PAYE scheme size or reference	Staging date
120,000 or more	1 October 2012
50,000–119,999	1 November 2012
30,000–49,999	1 January 2013
20,000–29,999	1 February 2013
10,000–19,999	1 March 2013
6000–9999	1 April 2013
4100–5999	1 May 2013
4000–4099	1 June 2013
3000–3999	1 July 2013
2000–2999	1 August 2013
1250–1999	1 September 2013
800–1249	1 October 2013
500–799	1 November 2013
350–499	1 January 2014
250–349	1 February 2014
160–249	1 April 2014
90–159	1 May 2014
62–89	1 July 2014
61	1 August 2014
60	1 October 2014
59	1 November 2014
58	1 January 2015
54–57	1 March 2015

PAYE scheme size or reference	Staging date
50–53	1 April 2015
Fewer than 30 with the last 2 characters in their PAYE reference numbers 92, A1–A9, B1–B9, AA–AZ, BA–BW, M1–M9, MA–MZ, Z1–Z9, ZA–ZZ , 0A–0Z, 1A–1Z or 2A–2Z	1 June 2015
Fewer than 30 with the last 2 characters in their PAYE reference number BX	1 July 2015
40–49	1 August 2015
Fewer than 30 with the last 2 characters in their PAYE reference number BY	1 September 2015
30–39	1 October 2015
Fewer than 30 with the last 2 characters in their PAYE reference number BZ	1 November 2015
Fewer than 30 with the last 2 characters in their PAYE reference numbers 02–04, C1–C9, D1–D9, CA–CZ or DA–DZ	1 January 2016
Fewer than 30 with the last 2 characters in their PAYE reference numbers 00 05–07, E1–E9 or EA–EZ	1 February 2016
Fewer than 30 with the last 2 characters in their PAYE reference numbers 01, 08–11, F1–F9, G1–G9, FA–FZ or GA–GZ	1 March 2016
Fewer than 30 with the last 2 characters in their PAYE reference numbers 12–16, 3A–3Z, H1–H9 or HA–HZ	1 April 2016
Fewer than 30 with the last 2 characters in their PAYE reference numbers I1–I9 or IA–IZ	1 May 2016
Fewer than 30 with the last 2 characters in their PAYE reference numbers 17–22, 4A–4Z, J1–J9 or JA–JZ	1 June 2016
Fewer than 30 with the last 2 characters in their PAYE reference numbers 23–29, 5A–5Z, K1–K9 or KA–KZ	1 July 2016

PAYE scheme size or reference	Staging date
Fewer than 30 with the last 2 characters in their PAYE reference numbers 30–37, 6A–6Z, L1–L9 or LA–LZ	1 August 2016
Fewer than 30 with the last 2 characters in their PAYE reference numbers N1–N9 or NA–NZ	1 September 2016
Fewer than 30 with the last 2 characters in their PAYE reference numbers 38–46, 7A–7Z, O1–O9 or OA–OZ	1 October 2016
Fewer than 30 with the last 2 characters in their PAYE reference numbers 47–57, 8A–8Z, Q1–Q9, R1–R9, S1–S9, T1–T9, QA–QZ, RA–RZ, SA–SZ or TA–TZ	1 November 2016
Fewer than 30 with the last 2 characters in their PAYE reference numbers 58–69, 9A–9Z, U1–U9, V1–V9, W1–W9, UA–UZ, VA–VZ or WA–WZ	1 January 2017
Fewer than 30 with the last 2 characters in their PAYE reference numbers 70–83, X1–X9, Y1–Y9, XA–XZ or YA–YZ	1 February 2017
Fewer than 30 with the last 2 characters in their PAYE reference numbers P1–P9 or PA–PZ	1 March 2017
Fewer than 30 with the last 2 characters in their PAYE reference numbers 84–91, 93–99	1 April 2017
Fewer than 30 unless otherwise described	1 April 2017
Employer who does not have a PAYE scheme	1 April 2017
New employer (PAYE income first payable between 1 April 2012 and 31 March 2013)	1 May 2017
New employer (PAYE income first payable between 1 April 2013 and 31 March 2014)	1 July 2017
New employer (PAYE income first payable between 1 April 2014 and 31 March 2015)	1 August 2017
New employer (PAYE income first payable between 1 April 2015 and 31 December 2015)	1 October 2017
New employer (PAYE income first payable between 1 January 2016 and 30 September 2016)	1 November 2017

PAYE scheme size or reference	Staging date
New employer (PAYE income first payable between 1 October 2016 and 30 June 2017)	1 January 2018
New employer (PAYE income first payable between 1 July 2017 and 30 September 2017)	1 February 2018

Source: Now Pensions website (*www.nowpensions.com/auto-enrolment-staging-dates*).

The following two links provide further detailed information.

www.thepensionsregulator.gov.uk/press/pn15-09.aspx
www.thepensionsregulator.gov.uk/docs/detailed-guidance-2.pdf

CHAPTER 5

Social Security Data

Jobseeker's Allowance

Jobseeker's Allowance (JSA) is payable to unemployed people who are actively seeking employment.

Unlike most benefits, JSA includes both a contributory and a means tested element based on the individual and their partner's income and savings. If an individual is eligible for Universal Credit, he or she may also be able to claim another type of contribution-based JSA, called "new style JSA". New style JSA works in the same way as contribution-based JSA.

To qualify for contributory JSA the claimant must have:

- actually paid Class 1 National Insurance contributions on earnings of at least 25 times the lower earnings level in one of the last two complete tax years prior to the benefit year in which the claim commences
- paid, or been credited, with Class 1 contributions on earnings of at least 50 times the lower earnings limit in each of the last two complete tax years.

Earnings on which Class 1 contributions are treated as paid at the nil% rate (ie where earnings are not less than the lower earnings limit but are less than the earnings threshold) are treated as earnings on which contributions were actually paid. A benefit year starts on the first Sunday in January.

To qualify for income-based JSA the claimant must:

- not have capital in excess of £16,000 (if he or she has capital of £6000 or more, a tariff of £1 is deducted for every £250 over the £6000 threshold)
- not be in paid work for 16 hours or more per week on average and nor may his or her partner be in paid work for 24 hours or more per week on average
- if under 18, show he or she is living away from home and in severe hardship.

SOCIAL SECURITY DATA

Rates of Contributory JSA

From	Claimant aged		
	25 or over	18 to 24	16 or 17
9 April 2018	£73.10	£57.90	£57.90
10 April 2017	£73.10	£57.90	£57.90
11 April 2016	£73.10	£57.90	£57.90
6 April 2015	£73.10	£57.90	£57.90
7 April 2014	£72.40	£57.35	£57.35
8 April 2013	£71.70	£56.80	£56.80
9 April 2012	£71.00	£56.25	£56.25
11 April 2011	£67.50	£53.45	£53.45

Main Points

- Contributory JSA is payable for a maximum of 182 days.
- Income-based JSA is payable for an indefinite period so long as the claimant remains eligible.
- All claimants (save a few exceptions) must agree and sign a Jobseeker's Agreement as a condition of receiving benefit.
- Claimants must take such steps as can be reasonably expected to secure employment.
- There is a prescribed list of those who are eligible for income support. Those who are not eligible will need to claim JSA instead.
- There is an age limit to JSA, currently 60 for women and 65 for men.
- Contributory JSA is payable at a flat rate and there are no additional amounts for dependants. Income-based JSA is means tested and additional amounts are payable for dependants.
- A claimant is not entitled to JSA for the first three waiting days, unless he or she is:
  - under 18 and falls into the severe hardship categories
  - in receipt of incapacity benefit or carer's allowance in the 12 weeks prior to the claim.
- A claimant must be available to take up any employment immediately and must be able to work 40 hours per week.
- A claimant may restrict the type of work he or she is prepared to accept provided he or she can still demonstrate reasonable prospects of

finding employment. However, after six months, he or she cannot place restrictions on the level of remuneration he or she is prepared to accept.
- Benefit can be withheld for four weeks (rising to 13 weeks for a second or third refusal or failure) if the claimant refuses:
  - to accept a job offer
  - or fails to follow a direction from the employment officer
  - or fails to take up a place on a training scheme or employment programme.
- Benefit can be withheld for 13 weeks (rising to 26 weeks and 156 weeks on the second and third failures) if the claimant:
  - has lost employment through misconduct
  - leaves employment voluntarily without just cause
  - fails to apply for, or accept, a reasonable offer of a job or participate in mandatory work activity.
- JSA is taxable. However, tax is not deducted at source but is recouped through PAYE if the person returns to work or at the end of the tax year from any tax refund due.

Employment and Support Allowance

Employment and Support Allowance (ESA) is payable to those unable to work through sickness or disability where the claim arose on or after 27 October 2008. It replaces Incapacity Benefit. Employees are usually entitled to Statutory Sick Pay (SSP) but may transfer to ESA if they are not entitled to SSP.

Eligibility

ESA includes both a contributory (known as "new style" ESA if entitled to claim Universal Credit) and a means-tested element.

To qualify for contributions-based ESA, the claimant must have:
- paid sufficient Class 1 or Class 2 contributions to confer an earnings factor of at least 25 times he lower earnings level in any one of the three tax years preceding the benefit year
- been paid or credited with sufficient Class 1 or Class 2 contributions to confer an earnings factor of at least 50 times the lower earnings level in each of the two tax years ending before the start of the benefit year.

Earnings on which Class 1 contributions are treated as paid at the nil% rate (ie where earnings are not less than the lower earnings limit but are less than the employee's earnings threshold) are treated as earnings on which contributions are actually paid.

To qualify for income-related ESA, the claimant must not have capital in excess of £16,000 (if he or she has capital of £6000 or over a tariff of £1 is deducted for every £250 over the £6000 threshold).

An individual can apply for "new style" ESA if entitled to apply for Universal Credit. An individual is entitled if either a single person anywhere in England, Wales and Scotland or a couple or family living in a Universal Credit area. New style ESA works in the same way as contribution-based ESA. Any partner's income and savings will not affect how much new style ESA is paid. New style ESA is payable on its own or at the same time as Universal Credit. If both are paid at the same time, the new style ESA payment will be deducted from the Universal Credit payment.

From	Basic allowance			Work-related activity component	Support component
	Assessment phase				
	Age 16–24	Age 25 or over	Main phase		
9 April 2018	£57.90	£73.10	£73.10	£29.05	£37.65
10 April 2017	£57.90	£73.10	£73.10	£29.05	£36.55
6 April 2016	£57.90	£73.10	£73.10	£29.05	£36.20
6 April 2015	£57.90	£73.10	£73.10	£29.05	£36.20
7 April 2014	£57.35	£72.40	£72.40	£28.75	£35.75
8 April 2013	£56.80	£71.70	£71.70	£28.45	£34.80
9 April 2012	£56.25	£71.00	£71.00	£28.15	£34.05
11 April 2011	£53.45	£67.50	£67.50	£26.75	£32.35

Main Points

- The claimant must:
  - be at least 16 years old
  - have limited capability for work
  - not be over pensionable age, not receiving SSP or SMP and not returned to work
  - not be entitled to Income Support or JSA.
- ESA is not paid for the first three "waiting days".
- Contributory ESA is paid at the assessment rate during the first 13 weeks.

- During the assessment phase, the claimant's capability to work is assessed.
- If the claimant is assessed as capable of working ESA is not paid.
- If the claimant is assessed as having limited capability to work, he or she will be paid the work-related activity component and supported back to work.
- If the claimant is assessed as having a severe illness or disability, he or she will be paid the support component and will not be required to undertake work-related activities as long as the condition subsists.
- If the claimant is terminally ill, the support component is payable from the first day of the claim.
- Income-related ESA may be paid if the claimant is not entitled to contributory ESA, or as a top up, if the claimant's income is low enough.
- Contributory ESA is taxable.

Incapacity Benefit

Incapacity benefit is payable to those unable to work through sickness or disability where the claim first arose before 27 October 2008. Employees are usually entitled to SSP instead.

Eligibility

To qualify for incapacity benefit the claimant must have:

- actually paid sufficient Class 1 or Class 2 National Insurance contributions to confer an earnings factor of at least 25 times the lower earnings level in one of the last three complete tax years prior to the benefit year in which the claim commences
- paid or been credited with sufficient Class 1 or Class 2 contributions to confer an earnings factor of at least 50 times the lower earnings level in each of the last two complete tax years.

Earnings on which Class 1 contributions are treated as paid at the nil% rate (ie where earnings are not less than the lower earnings limit but are less than the earnings threshold) are treated as earnings on which contributions were actually paid.

Rates for Incapacity Benefit

| From | Long-term benefit | | | Short-term benefit | | |
| | Basic | Higher | Lower | Lower rate | Higher rate | Over pension age |
		Age addition				
9 April 2018	£109.60	£11.60	£6.45	£82.65	£97.85	£105.15
10 April 2017	£106.40	£11.25	£6.25	£80.25	£95.00	£102.10
6 April 2016	£105.35	£11.15	£6.20	£79.45	£94.05	£101.10
6 April 2015	£105.35	£11.15	£6.20	£79.45	£94.05	£101.10
7 April 2014	£104.10	£11.00	£6.15	£78.50	£92.95	£99.90
8 April 2013	£101.35	£10.70	£6.00	£76.45	£90.50	£97.25
9 April 2012	£99.15	£11.70	£5.90	£74.80	£88.55	95.15
11 April 2011	£94.25	£13.80	£5.60	£71.10	£84.15	£90.45

Main Points

- The claimant must be incapable of work through physical or mental sickness or disability.
- The claimant must have been under the age of 65 when the period of incapacity to work started.
- A claimant is not entitled to incapacity benefit for the first three "waiting days".
- Incapacity benefit is payable at three rates, the short-term lower rate for the first 28 weeks, the short-term higher rate between weeks 29 and 52, and the long-term rate after 52 weeks.
- Short-term incapacity benefit is payable at a special rate to claimants over State pension age.
- Short-term incapacity benefit paid at the lower rate, or at the rate for pensioners during the first 28 weeks, is not taxable. The benefit is taxable after the first 28 weeks.

Maternity Payments

Present Regulations

An employed woman who becomes pregnant is usually entitled to Statutory Maternity Pay (SMP). If she is not entitled to SMP, she may be eligible for Maternity Allowance.

To be eligible for Maternity Allowance, the claimant must have been employed or self-employed in 26 of the 66 weeks before the expected week of childbirth (EWC), and her average earnings must have been at least equal to the Maternity Allowance (MA) threshold.

MA is paid at 90% of the average weekly earnings, but not exceeding the standard rate. (Weekly earnings are taken to be equal to the lower earnings limit for each week that a Class 2 NIC is paid.) It is paid for up to 39 weeks but payment will stop earlier if the woman returns to work or she agrees that her partner should take shared parental leave and claim statutory shared parental pay.

If a woman is neither employed nor self-employed but is married or in a civil partnership, and for at least 26 weeks out of the 66 weeks before the baby is due she has carried out unpaid work for her spouse or civil partner's self-employment, then MA may be paid for 14 weeks. This applies for babies due on or after 27 July 2014.

Maternity Allowance Rates

From	Standard rate	Maternity allowance threshold
9 April 2018	£145.18	£30.00
10 April 2017	£140.98	£30.00
6 April 2016	£139.58	£30.00
6 April 2015	£139.58	£30.00
7 April 2014	£138.18	£30.00
8 April 2013	£136.78	£30.00
1 April 2012	£135.45	£30.00
3 April 2011	£128.73	£30.00

Maternity Grant (Social Fund)

A sure start maternity grant is payable from the Social Fund to a woman who, or whose partner, is receiving income support, income-based Jobseeker's Allowance, income-related ESA, pension credit, Child Tax Credit or Working Tax Credit that includes a disability or severe disability element or Universal Credit.

Rate for Sure Start Maternity Grant

Baby expected, born or adopted from	Amount
16 June 2002	£500

Other Benefits

Means-tested Benefits

The following other benefits are means tested:
- pension credit
- income support
- income-based Jobseeker's Allowance
- housing benefit
- council tax benefit.

In addition, further grants or loans may be made from the Social Fund for specific needs.

Pension credit is an income-related benefit made up of two parts — guarantee credit and savings credit.

Guarantee credit tops up weekly income. Savings credit is an extra payment for people who saved some money towards their retirement, for example, a pension.

Income support tops up actual earnings (as defined) to an applicable amount, which comprises a personal allowance, premiums and housing costs. Income-based Jobseeker's Allowance replaced income support for the unemployed, and is calculated on similar lines.

Housing benefit and council tax benefit provide help with housing costs and council tax for claimants of other means-tested benefits. Housing benefit will be replaced by universal credit.

Social Fund payments are paid on a non-discretionary basis for funeral payments and cold weather payments. They are paid on a discretionary and budget-limited basis for other purposes.

Non Means-tested Benefits

Non means-tested benefits are either contributory or non-contributory. Contributory benefits depend on sufficient National Insurance contributions being paid or credited for entitlement.

Contributory benefits are:

- incapacity benefit
- jobseeker's allowance (contributions based)
- maternity allowance
- retirement pension
- bereavement allowance
- bereavement payment
- widowed parent's allowance
- widowed mother's allowance (if widowed before 9 April 2001)
- widow's pension (if widowed before 9 April 2001)
- widow's payment (if widowed before 9 April 2001).

Non-contributory benefits are:

- attendance allowance
- child benefit (including one-parent benefit)
- disability living allowance (being replaced by) personal independence payments)
- guardian's allowance
- industrial death benefit (for deaths before 11 April 1988)
- industrial disablement benefit
- carer's allowance
- personal independence payments (replacing disability living allowance)
- pneumoconiosis, byssinosis, etc benefit
- retirement pension (non-contributory)
- severe disablement allowance
- war pension.

Tax Credits

In October 1999 two of the social security benefits were replaced by tax credits. Family credit was replaced by the working families tax credit, and disability working allowance was replaced by the disabled person's tax credit. These tax credits were paid to workers on low earnings. Although administered by HMRC, employers were responsible for paying the tax credits to employees from 6 April 2000.

These two tax credits were replaced by two new tax credits on 6 April 2003. The working tax credit is payable to workers with low earnings, while the child tax credit is payable to low income families with children, irrespective of whether the claimant and/or his or her partner is working. Tax credits will be replaced by universal credit. Tax credits are now paid directly by HMRC to the claimant's bank account. Working tax credit was previously paid by the employer through the payroll, but this was phased out during 2005/06.

Working Tax Credit

The working tax credit is payable from 6 April 2003 to top-up earnings. The main rules of the tax credit are as follows.

- The claimant must be either:
  - aged 16 or over, working for at least 16 hours per week and either he or his partner has responsibility for a child or has a disability which puts him or her at a disadvantage in the job market, or
  - aged 25 or over and working for at least 30 hours per week.
- The tax credit comprises a basic credit; additional credits for a partner; being a lone parent; working 30 hours or more per week and for having a disability.
- The 30 hours or more credit can be obtained if the claimant or his partner works at least 30 hours, or if they work more than 30 hours in aggregate, one works for more than 16 hours per week, and they have responsibility for a child.
- A childcare tax credit of 70% of eligible childcare costs may be claimed, up to maximum costs of £175 for one child or £300 for two or more children.
- If the claimant's income exceeds the income threshold the award is scaled down by 41% of the excess.
- The award is initially based on the previous year's income, and may be revised after the end of the tax year. It will only be reduced due to an increase in income if the increase is more than £2500. The credit is normally awarded for a whole tax year, but may be varied if circumstances change.

Annual Rates of Maximum Working Tax Credit

	2011/ 12	2012/ 13	2013/ 14	2014/ 15	2015/ 16	2016/ 17	2017/ 18	2018/ 19
Basic element	£1920	£1920	£1920	£1960	£1960	£1960	£1960	£1960
Additional adult element	£1950	£1950	£1970	£1990	£2010	£2010	£2010	£2010
Lone parent element	£1950	£1950	£1970	£1990	£2010	£2010	£2010	£2010
30 hours element	£790	£790	£790	£800	£810	£810	£810	£810
Disabled worker element	£2650	£2790	£2855	£2935	£2970	£2970	£3000	£3090
Enhanced disabled adult element	£1130	£1190	£1220	£1255	£1275	£1275	£1290	£1330
50 plus return to work payment 16–29 hours	£1365	—	—	—	—	—	—	—
50 plus return to work payment 30+ hours	£2030	—	—	—	—	—	—	—
Income threshold	£6420	£6420	£6420	£6420	£6420	£6420	£6420	£6420
Withdrawal rate	41%	41%	41%	41%	41%	41%	41%	41%

Child Tax Credit

The child tax credit is payable from 6 April 2003 to low income families with children. The main rules of the tax credit are as follows.

- The claimant must be responsible for a child (up to 31 August following their 16th birthday) or qualifying young person (aged under 20 and in full-time education, not being advanced education).
- Where more than one person has responsibility, the claim may be made by the person who has the main responsibility. They may elect which person should be treated as having the main responsibility.
- The tax credit comprises a family credit; additional credits for each child; credits for disabled children.
- If the claimant's income exceeds the first income threshold the award is scaled down by 41% of the excess. This is after taking into account any scaling down of the working tax credit.

- The award is initially based on the previous year's income and may be revised after the end of the tax year; it will only be reduced due to an increase in income if the increase is more than £2500. The credit is normally awarded for a whole tax year, but may be varied if circumstances change.

Annual Rates of Maximum Child Tax Credit

	2011/ 12	2012/ 13	2013/ 14	2014/ 15	2015/ 16	2016/ 17	2017/ 18	2018/ 19
Family element	£545	£545	£545	£545	£545	£545	£545	£545
Family element, baby addition	—	—	—	—	—	—	—	—
Child element (per child)	£2555	£2690	£2720	£2750	£2780	£2780	£2780	£2780
Disabled child additional element (per child)	£2800	£2950	£3015	£3100	£3140	£3140	£3175	£3275
Enhanced disabled child additional element (per child)	£1130	£1190	£1220	£1255	£1275	£1275	£1290	£1325
First income threshold	£15,860	£15,860	£15,910	£16,010	£16,105	£16,105	£16,105	£16,105
Withdrawal rate	41%	41%	41%	41%	41%	41%	41%	41%
Second income threshold	£40,000	—	—	—	—	—	—	—
Withdrawal rate	41%	—	—	—	—	—	—	—

CHAPTER 6

Employment Law

Recruitment

Generally, an employer is free to engage whoever it wishes to a job, and may use any selection process it wants to. However, the following points should be noted.

Discrimination

- It is unlawful to discriminate against someone who has one or more of the "protected characteristics" set out in the **Equality Act 2010** viz: age, disability, gender reassignment, marriage and civil partnership, pregnancy and maternity, race, religion or belief, sex and sexual orientation.
- It is unlawful to treat a person less favourably than someone else (eg by not offering a job, even if that person is the best-qualified candidate) because he or she is associated with a person who has a protected characteristic (eg a disabled person). This is known as *discrimination by association*.
- It is unlawful to treat a person less favourably than someone else (eg by not offering the job, even where that person is the best-qualified candidate) because the employer believes mistakenly that he or she has a protected characteristic (eg the employer thinks that the applicant is gay). This is known as *discrimination by perception*.
- It is unlawful — except in very limited circumstances — to ask questions about a candidate's health or disability, including about someone's sickness absence record. Nor can anyone else (eg an occupational health practitioner) ask these questions on the employer's behalf. Such

questions can only be asked once the person has been offered the post or made a conditional offer.

- It is unlawful to treat part-time workers (ie employees as well as other workers) less favourably than comparable full-time workers working in the same establishment.
- It is unlawful to treat fixed-term employees less favourably than comparable permanent employees working in the same establishment.
- The employer can recruit a job candidate or promote an existing employee because he or she has a particular protected characteristic if he or she is of equal merit to another candidate/employee under consideration and the employer reasonably thinks that people with that characteristic are under-represented in the workforce, or suffer a disadvantage connected to that characteristic. The employer can only take such positive action where it is a proportionate way of addressing the under-representation or disadvantage. The employer is not allowed to choose a less suitable candidate/employee just because the individual has a protected characteristic that is under-represented or disadvantaged. Taking any form of positive action is entirely voluntary.

Women

Legislation restricting the employment of new and expectant mothers, and of women of childbearing age, is designed to ensure their continued health and safety and, where appropriate, that of their babies or developing foetuses. Thus, the following provisions apply.

- "No woman or girl may be employed in a factory or workshop within four weeks after she has given birth to a child" (s.205, **Public Health Act 1936**).
- "An employee entitled to ordinary maternity leave must not work, or be permitted by her employer to work, during the period of two weeks which commences with the day on which childbirth occurs" (regulation 8, **Maternity and Parental Leave Regulations 1999**).
- A woman "of reproductive capacity" must not be employed in any lead smelting or refining process or in any lead-acid battery manufacturing process; nor may she be employed in the cleaning of any place where any such processes are carried out (regulation 4(2) and schedule 1, **Control of Lead at Work Regulations 2002**).
- Employers must ensure that a woman "of reproductive capacity" is not exposed to ionising radiation in excess of 13mSv in any consecutive period of three months (regulation 24 and schedule 4, **Ionising Radiations Regulations 1999**).

- Where women of childbearing age are employed in an undertaking, and the work is of a kind which could involve risk to the health and safety of a new or expectant mother or to that of her baby from any processes or working conditions, or physical, biological or chemical agents, the risk assessment required by regulation 3(1) of the **Management of Health and Safety at Work Regulations 1999** must include an assessment of such risk. If, in the case of an individual employee, there is little the employer can do to avoid that risk, the employer must either offer her suitable alternative work to do (which she must not unreasonably refuse) or suspend her from work on full pay for so long as is necessary to prevent that risk (regulation 16, **Management of Health and Safety at Work Regulations 1999**; regulation 8, **Merchant Shipping and Fishing Vessels (Health and Safety at Work) Regulations 1997** and ss.66–70, **Employment Rights Act 1996**).
- A new or expectant mother who works at night must either be transferred to suitable alternative work during the day or be suspended from work on full pay (for so long as is necessary) if, on the advice of her doctor or registered midwife, her employment at night is damaging to her health or that of her child or developing foetus (regulation 17, **Management of Health and Safety at Work Regulations 1999** and ss.66–70, **Employment Rights Act 1996**).
- A member of an aircraft flight crew who has reason to believe she is pregnant must notify her employers in writing without delay. Once her pregnancy is confirmed, she is deemed to be suspended from work and may only resume her duties during the initial stages of her pregnancy if it is considered safe for her to do so and certain conditions are met. One of the employer's duties is to ensure that the woman's exposure to cosmic radiation during her pregnancy remains below the limits laid down in the relevant legislation.

Employers should note that they are duty-bound to provide suitable rest facilities for those of their employees who are pregnant or breastfeeding (regulation 25(4), **Workplace (Health, Safety and Welfare) Regulations 1992**).

Young Persons

A "young person" is a person over compulsory school age but under the age of 18.

Under the **Management of Health and Safety at Work Regulations 1999**, employers must not employ any young person in any capacity unless they have first assessed the risks to the health and safety of young persons generally, taking particular account of:

* their inexperience and immaturity, and lack of awareness of workplace risks
* the fitting-out and layout of the workplace
* the nature, degree and duration of exposure to physical, biological and chemical agents
* the form, range and use of work equipment and the way in which it is handled
* the organisation of processes and activities
* the extent of the health and safety training provided, or to be provided, to young persons
* risks from agents, processes and work listed in the Annex to Council Directive 94/33/EC "on the protection of young people at work".

Young persons may not carry out, except in certain limited circumstances, work which:

* is beyond their physical or psychological capacity
* involves exposure to carcinogens, toxic substances, teratogens or substances causing heritable damage
* involves exposure to radiation
* involves a risk of accidents which a young person could not have recognised or avoided due to lack of experience or training
* involves extremes of cold or heat and is a risk to health
* involves noise and is a risk to health
* involves vibration and is a risk to health.

Young persons may only carry out work in these categories if it is necessary for their training, they are supervised by a competent person, and any risk is reduced to the lowest level that is reasonably practicable.

Young persons are also prohibited from certain sorts of work under the **Control of Lead at Work Regulations 2002** and the **Ionising Radiations Regulations 1999**.

Under the **Working Time Regulations 1998** (as amended), young persons aged 16 and 17, who have lawfully left school, must not be permitted to work for more than 40 hours in any week (including overtime hours) or for more than eight hours on any day. Nor may they be permitted to work at night during the "restricted period" (that is to say, between 2200 and 0600 or, if their contracts require them to work after 2200, between 2300 and 0700).

Save for an absolute prohibition on their employment between midnight and 0400, these restrictions do not apply to young persons working in agriculture, postal or newspaper deliveries, retail trading, bakeries, catering businesses, hotels, restaurants, public houses or bars:

(a) if their employment after 2200 (or 2300, as the case may be) is necessary to maintain continuity of service or production or to respond to a surge in demand for a product or service

(b) if there are no adult workers available to do the work

(c) if performing the work would not adversely affect their education or training

(d) if they are permitted to take their normal rest breaks and rest periods or equivalent periods of compensatory rest.

Young persons must be afforded free health and capabilities assessments before being assigned to night work and follow-up assessments should be carried out at regular intervals. If a doctor certifies that a young worker is suffering from health problems associated with his or her work at night, the employer must, if possible, transfer that worker to suitable alternative work during the day.

Young persons must be allowed a minimum 12-hour work-free break in every period of 24 consecutive hours, two consecutive work-free rest days in every week (a week being the period from Monday–Sunday, inclusive) and a minimum of 30-minute rest break in the course of any working day or shift lasting (or expected to last) for more than four and a half hours.

Children

In law, a child is a person who is not over compulsory school age. In England and Wales, children who turn 16 during a school year must remain at school until the last Friday in June. A child whose 16th birthday falls after the last Friday in June but before the beginning of the next school year may likewise leave school on that same last Friday in June. In Scotland, children whose 16th birthdays fall between 1 March and 30 September may leave school on 31 May of that same year; while those whose 16th birthdays fall outside that period must remain at school until the first day of the Christmas holiday break.

The **Children and Young Persons Act 1933** and **Children and Young Persons Act 1963** (as amended) state that no child shall be employed:

- so long as he or she is under the age of 14 years
- to do any work other than light work (see below)
- before the close of school hours on any day on which he or she is required to attend school
- before seven o'clock in the morning or after seven o'clock in the evening on any day

- for more than two hours on any day on which he or she is required to attend school
- for more than two hours on any Sunday
- for more than eight hours or, if he or she is under the age of 15, for more than five hours on any day (other than a Sunday) on which he or she is *not* required to attend school
- for more than 12 hours in any week in which he or she is required to attend school
- for more than 35 hours or, if under the age of 15, for more than 25 hours in any week in which he or she is *not* required to attend school
- for more than four consecutive hours in any day without a rest break of one hour
- at any time in a year unless, at that time, he or she has had, or could still have, during school holidays, at least two consecutive weeks without employment.

The expression "light work" means work of a kind that is unlikely to affect the safety, health or development of a school-age child or to interfere with the child's education or regular and punctual attendance at school.

Local authority bye-laws

Under local authority bye-laws, which may vary slightly from authority to authority, school children must not be employed in any of the following occupations.

1. In the kitchen of any hotel, cook shop, fried fish shop, restaurant, snack bar or cafeteria.
2. As a marker or attendant in any billiards or pools saloon, licensed gaming house or registered club.
3. In, or in connection with, the sale of alcohol, except where alcohol is sold exclusively in sealed containers.
4. Collecting or sorting rags, scrap metal or refuse.
5. As a fairground attendant or assistant in any slaughterhouse.
6. In, or in connection with, any racecourse or race track, or other place where any like sport is carried on.
7. In any heavy agricultural work.
8. In, or in connection with, the sale of paraffin, turpentine, white spirit, methylated spirit or petroleum spirit.
9. Touting or selling from door to door.
10. As a window cleaner.

Copies of local authority bye-laws are available on request from the relevant local authority for the district in which the would-be employer conducts its business.

Other prohibited occupations
Section 1(1) of the **Employment of Women, Young Persons and Children Act 1920** prohibits the employment of any child in an "industrial undertaking", which includes particularly:

- mines and quarries
- industries in which articles are manufactured, altered, cleaned, repaired, ornamented, finished, adapted for sale, broken up or demolished or in which materials are transformed
- construction, reconstruction, maintenance, repair, alteration or demolition of any building, railway, harbour, dock, pier, canal, inland waterway, road, tunnel, bridge, viaduct, sewer, drain, well, gaswork, waterwork or other work of construction, including the preparation for or laying the foundations of any such work or structure
- transport of passengers or goods by road, rail or inland waterway, including the handling of goods at docks, quays, wharves and warehouses but excluding transport by hand.

The 1920 Act cautions that the relevant local authority (in Scotland, the education authority) must be consulted if the employer is in any doubt about the lines or divisions between industry, commerce and agriculture.

Procedure
An employer wishing to employ a school-age child (in whatever capacity) must first apply to the relevant local education authority for an Employment Certificate. The authority will supply an application form on request, together with a copy of its bye-laws relating to the employment of children. The application form must be completed and returned to the authority within seven days of the date on which the child's employment began, and must be signed by one or other of the child's parents or legal guardians consenting to the child being employed in the undertaking in question and confirming that he or she is medically fit to carry out the duties described. The employer must also provide the parent or guardian with relevant and comprehensible information about any health and safety risks associated with the job in question. That information must include particulars about the preventive and protective measures the employer proposes to adopt (or has already put in place) to eliminate or minimise those risks (regulation 10(2), **Management of Health and Safety at Work Regulations 1999**).

Work experience

Under the **Education Act 1996**, the restrictions otherwise imposed on the employment of school-age children (in relation to working hours and periods of employment) do not apply during the last two years of compulsory schooling if the employment in question is part of a local authority-approved work experience programme. The Act does not, however, permit the employment of such children in work otherwise prohibited by statute or local authority bye-laws.

Migrant Workers

Employers are under a requirement to check all prospective and ongoing employees' entitlement to work in the UK, or they risk breaking the law under the **Immigration, Asylum and Nationality Act 2006** (see below). The Home Office operates a points-based immigration procedure governing the way individuals from outside the European Economic Area (EEA) and Switzerland can work, train and study in the UK. It is based on a points-based system and an employer-led sponsorship licence system.

Points-based system

The points-based system only covers migrants from outside the EEA and Switzerland. If an employer wants to employ or teach an EEA or Swiss national, it should be able to do this without needing the permission of the UK Border Agency.

Croatian nationals are, however, required to have a certificate of sponsorship under Tier 2 of the points-based system in order to commence working in the UK. They must also apply for an accession worker card before they can begin employment. Once they have worked lawfully in the UK for 12 months, they are free to continue to work without restrictions.

The previous restrictions on employing Romanian and Bulgarian nationals were lifted with effect from 1 January 2014.

The EEA consists of Austria, Belgium, Bulgaria, Croatia, Cyprus, Czech Republic, Denmark, Estonia, Finland, France, Germany, Greece, Hungary, Iceland, Ireland, Italy, Latvia, Liechtenstein, Lithuania, Luxembourg, Malta, the Netherlands, Norway, Poland, Portugal, Romania, Slovakia, Slovenia, Spain, Sweden and the UK (ie all the EU countries plus Iceland, Norway and Liechtenstein).

Under the points-based system, migrants need to pass a points-based assessment before they are given permission to enter or remain in the UK. The system consists of five tiers. Each tier has different points requirements.

The number of points the migrant needs and the way the points are awarded will depend on the tier he or she is applying under. Points are awarded to reflect the migrant's ability, experience, age and when appropriate the level of need within the sector the migrant will be working.

For Tiers 2 and 5, points are awarded for a valid certificate of sponsorship from a UK employer.

As from April 2017, employers that employ non-EEA nationals under Tier 2 are subject to a visa levy, referred to as the "immigration skills charge".

The points-based system consists of five tiers.

Tier 1   High-value migrants, for whom no job offer or sponsoring employer is required.

Tier 2   Skilled workers with proven English language ability who have a job offer, eg teachers, nurses and engineers.

Tier 3   Low skilled workers filling specific temporary labour shortages.

Tier 4   Students.

Tier 5   Youth mobility and temporary workers, eg musicians coming to play in a concert.

Tier 3 is suspended indefinitely because most low-skilled jobs are currently capable of being filled by EEA nationals.

As from 6 April 2011, the Government imposed annual limits on the number of non-EU migrants who can be admitted into the UK to work under Tier 2.

Before an employer can recruit a worker from outside the EEA into a Tier 2 post, it must advertise the job in an approved medium in the UK for a period of not less than four weeks. Additionally, employers must in most cases advertise the post through Jobcentre Plus Universal Jobmatch.

Overseas workers who want to transfer to the UK base of their company under Tier 2 must have worked for that company for at least one year. In order to be able to stay in the UK for more than 12 months, the individual must have a minimum salary of £41,500 and the stay will be limited to five years. For Tier 2 intra-company transfers of up to 12 months, the minimum salary threshold is £24,800.

Sponsors and licences
An employer-led sponsorship licence system has replaced the work permit system. Employers that wish to recruit and employ migrants from outside the EEA and Switzerland — or to extend the employment of an individual when his or her visa expires — are required to hold a

sponsorship licence and to issue certificates of sponsorship to migrants that they wish to employ.

The purposes of the sponsorship are to provide evidence that the migrant has a genuine job in the UK and acts as a pledge from the sponsor that he or she will accept the responsibilities of sponsorship in respect of the migrant.

Organisations that wish to recruit migrant workers under Tier 2, Tier 4 or Tier 5 need to apply to the UK Border Agency for a sponsorship licence by completing the online application form on the UK Government website *(www.gov.uk/apply-sponsor-licence)*. Under Tiers 2 and 5, Temporary Workers, the sponsor must be a UK-based employer. Under Tier 4, the sponsor must be a UK-based educational institution.

Migrants wishing to come to the UK under Tier 5: Youth Mobility do not require a UK-based employer.

The licence lasts for four years and the organisation must renew the licence prior to the expiry date to continue as sponsor.

Penalties

An employer's breach of the system described above can lead to a downgrading or removal of the sponsorship licence. The penalty on summary conviction under the **Immigration, Asylum and Nationality Act 2006** is a penalty fine of up to £20,000 for each offence (increased from £10,000 in May 2014). If an employer is found to have knowingly hired illegal workers, it could face an unlimited fine and imprisonment of individuals for up to two years.

Since the bringing into force of the **Immigration Act 2016** (in July 2016), overseas nationals who work in Britain without the requisite permission may also be liable to prosecution for illegal working, leading to a fine or custodial sentence.

The right to work in the UK

The work permit arrangement closed on 26 November 2008 and was replaced by Tier 2 of the points-based system (see above).

Under existing immigration rules, the following do not need permission in order to take up employment while in the UK.

• Nationals of the EEA (except nationals of Croatia (see above)). Prior to 1 May 2011, people from the Czech Republic, Estonia, Hungary, Latvia, Lithuania, Poland, Slovakia and Slovenia were required to register with the UK Border Agency under the Accession State Worker Registration Scheme if they planned to work for a UK employer for more than one month. This scheme is no longer operational.

- People born in Gibraltar.
- Swiss nationals.
- Ancestry visa holders, ie people born in a Commonwealth country who have a grandparent born in the UK.
- People who are spouses, unmarried partners or civil partners of UK or EEA nationals (whatever their own nationality) provided they have been granted visas confirming their status.
- Those whose spouses unmarried partners or civil partners are non-EEA nationals who have been granted permission to work in the UK — in which case, they may work for the same length of time as the spouse, partner or civil partner.
- Those with indefinite leave to remain in the UK.

Full details of these requirements are contained in the UK Border Agency booklet *Comprehensive Guidance for United Kingdom Employers on Changes to the Law on Preventing Illegal Working*. This is available at *www.ukba. homeoffice.gov.uk*

Further details on the changes introduced in 2010 can be found in the "Statement of changes to the immigration rules" also on this website.

Dismissal

Section 94 of the **Employment Rights Act 1996** states that every employee has the qualified right not to be unfairly dismissed. However, unless dismissed for an inadmissible or unlawful reason (see below), an employee does not qualify to pursue a complaint of unfair dismissal before an employment tribunal unless continuously employed for two years or more at the effective date of termination of his or her contract of employment.

The time limit for bringing a claim of unfair dismissal to tribunal is three months from the effective date of termination.

Meaning of Dismissal

There is a dismissal in law if:

- the contract under which an employee is employed is terminated by the employer (whether with or without notice)
- an employee is employed under a limited-term contract (ie a fixed-term or task-related contract) and that contract terminates by virtue of the limiting event without being renewed under the same contract, or

- an employee resigns, with or without notice, in circumstances such that he or she is entitled to resign without notice by reason of the employer's conduct (usually referred to as a "constructive dismissal").

Permitted Reasons for Dismissal

The **Employment Rights Act 1996** specifies five categories of potentially fair reasons for dismissal.

1. The capability or qualifications of the employee for performing the kind of work he or she was employed to do (this can include incompetence and ill health).
2. The employee's conduct.
3. Redundancy.
4. Continued employment would be illegal because of a statutory restriction.
5. Some other substantial reason (SOSR) of a kind such as to justify the dismissal of an employee holding the position which that employee held.

This is a "catch-all" category, designed to cover dismissals that do not fall into any of the previous categories but are nevertheless potentially fair. Examples include: dismissal because of an employee's refusal to accept changes in the terms and conditions of the employment contract, dismissal because of third party pressure and dismissal because of the breakdown of the mutual term of trust and confidence between employer and employee.

In tribunal proceedings, it is for the respondent employer to show the reason (or, if more than one, the principal reason) for the employee's dismissal and that it was one of the reasons listed above. It is then up to the tribunal to decide, on the evidence before it, whether the employer acted reasonably or unreasonably in treating that reason as a sufficient reason for dismissing the employee.

An employee held to have been unfairly dismissed will be awarded appropriate compensation. There are three elements to such an award. These are: the basic award (maximum: £15,240), the compensatory award (maximum: £83,682, or the equivalent of the claimant's annual salary, whichever is the lower, except for certain discrimination and whistleblowing cases) and, in circumstances in which an employer fails to comply (or comply fully) with an order for reinstatement or re-engagement, an additional award of between 26 and 52 weeks' pay, which is currently capped at a maximum of £508 per week (ie between £13,208 and £26,416).

Under the regime that came into force on 6 April 2009 the employment tribunal may, if it considers it just and equitable, increase (or decrease) an award by up to 25% if the Acas Code of Practice, *Disciplinary and Grievance Procedures* applies to the claim and the employer (or employee) has failed unreasonably to comply with the code. The maximum levels of compensation still apply, however, ie any uplift of up to 25% cannot result in an overall figure that exceeds the relevant cap.

Wrongful Dismissal

An employee will be treated as having been wrongfully dismissed if (in circumstances which do not justify summary dismissal) his or her employment is terminated without benefit of the notice to which he or she is entitled under his or her contract of employment. Breach of contract claims (arising out of, or outstanding on, the termination of an employee's employment) may be heard by the employment tribunals. Claims for damages in excess of £25,000 must, however, be lodged with the civil courts. Such claims may be pursued regardless of the claimant's age or length of service at the effective date of termination of his or her contract of employment.

Inadmissible and Unlawful Reasons for Dismissal

It is unlawful and automatically unfair to dismiss an employee (or select that employee for redundancy) on grounds of:
* race, colour, nationality, national or ethnic origin or religion or belief
* sex, gender reassignment or sexual orientation
* being married or having a civil partner
* pregnancy or maternity leave
* age
* disability.

There is no upper limit on the amount of compensation that may be awarded in such cases, although, in 2009, the EAT set out an updated version of the "bands" for an award for potential injury to feelings. These bands were uprated in line with inflation as from September 2017 as follows.
* Lower band — £800–£8400 (for less serious cases, eg a one-off minor incident.
* Middle band — £8400–£25,200 (for serious cases).
* Upper band — £25,200–£42,000 (for exceptionally severe cases, eg a lengthy campaign of serious harassment).

Only the most extreme cases would attract an award for injury to feelings in excess of £42,000.

A complaint of unlawful discrimination on such grounds may be presented to an employment tribunal regardless of the employee's age or length of service at the material time.

It is also unlawful and *prima facie* unfair to dismiss employees or select them for redundancy:

- because of their membership or non-membership of a trade union or participation in union activities at an appropriate time
- for asserting one or other of their statutory employment rights, or for challenging or questioning any alleged infringement of those rights (whether before an employment tribunal or otherwise)
- for reasons connected with a relevant transfer, ie the transfer or sale of the employer's business (or part of that business) or the purchase or acquisition of another employer's business
- for carrying out (or proposing to carry out) their functions as safety representatives, representatives of employee safety, employee representatives, pension scheme trustees, trade union officials, workforce representatives, information and consultation representatives or as members of a European Works Council (or Special Negotiating Body)
- for alerting their employers (in the absence of appointed or elected safety representatives or safety committees) to health and safety risks associated with their work or for leaving (or proposing to leave or refusing to return to the workplace) in circumstances of danger which they perceive to be serious or imminent
- for exercising their rights as protected or opted-out shop workers or betting workers not to work on Sundays
- for asserting (or refusing to forego) their rights under the **National Minimum Wage Act 1998**, the **Working Time Regulations 1998**, the **Part-time Workers (Prevention of Less Favourable Treatment) Regulations 2000** or the **Fixed-term Employees (Prevention of Less Favourable Treatment) Regulations 2002**
- for asserting or exercising their rights to maternity leave, adoption leave, parental leave, paternity leave, shared parental leave, time off for dependants or their right to apply for flexible working
- because they have been summoned for or have taken time off work for jury service
- for having made a protected disclosure within the meaning of the **Public Interest Disclosure Act 1998**

- for being entitled to the payment of working tax credits through the payroll (within the meaning of the **Tax Credits Act 2002**)
- while taking part in official industrial action during the protected period (ie the period of 12 weeks starting with the date on which the relevant strike or other industrial action began)
- on grounds concerned with the facilitation or prevention of trade union recognition
- for exercising the right to be accompanied at a formal disciplinary or grievance hearing (or seeking to do so)
- for applying for "time to train", being granted such a request or complaining about the right to make a request
- for exercising rights relating to transnational information and consultation of employees
- for exercising rights in connection with the **Agency Workers Regulations 2010**
- in respect of workers engaged on zero-hours contracts, for breaching a contractual exclusivity clause purporting to prevent them from working for another employer (in force since 11 January 2016).

Employees dismissed for any of the above reasons may pursue their complaints before the employment tribunals regardless of their respective ages or length of continuous employment at the material time (with the exception of those dismissed for reasons connected with a relevant transfer, in which case a minimum of two years' service is required).

In addition to the above provisions, since June 2013, any employee dismissed for a reason relating to his or her political opinion or affiliation may bring an unfair dismissal claim to tribunal irrespective of his or her length of service.

Additionally, as from 1 October 2014, employees serving in the reserve forces do not require the usual two-year period of qualifying service in order to bring a claim of unfair dismissal to tribunal where the reason for the dismissal was connected with their membership of the reserve forces.

Termination of Employment through a Settlement Agreement

As from 29 July 2013, the **Enterprise and Regulatory Reform Act 2013** introduced new provisions into the **Employment Rights Act 1996** permitting employers to offer employees a "settlement agreement" to terminate their employment, irrespective of whether any dispute between them has arisen. If the employee rejects the offer, and is subsequently dismissed, he or she is not permitted to use the fact that the employer made the offer at any tribunal hearing for unfair dismissal (unless something improper was said or done during the pre-termination negotiations). Similarly, the fact that the employer made a settlement offer cannot be grounds for a claim of constructive unfair dismissal.

The exclusion of pre-termination negotiations and settlement offers being admissible in evidence before an employment tribunal only applies, however, to claims for standard unfair dismissal. In the event of any other type of claim (including those for automatically unfair dismissal or unlawful discrimination), the claimant is able to present evidence about any pre-termination negotiations and/or settlement offered.

The Advisory, Conciliation and Arbitration Service (Acas) has published a statutory Code of Practice setting out the principles on the use of settlement agreements, together with accompanying non-statutory guidance.

Disciplinary and Grievance Procedures

The regime, which came into force on 6 April 2009 (and was updated in March 2015), is based on reasonable compliance with the revised Acas Code of Practice, *Disciplinary and Grievance Procedures*, which also came into effect on that date.

The Acas Code does not apply to redundancies, ill health dismissal or to the non-renewal of fixed-term contracts. Its scope is limited to disciplinary warnings, dismissals for misconduct and/or poor performance, some types of "some other substantial reason" dismissals and grievances. It is accompanied by non-statutory guidance.

The code states that the employer should follow the following sequence when applying disciplinary procedures to its employees (ie those working under a contract of employment — workers and the self-employed are not covered by the code).

1. Establish the facts of each case.
2. Inform the employee of the problem and advise of the right of accompaniment.
3. Hold a meeting with the employee to discuss the problem.
4. Decide appropriate action.
5. Advise the employee of the right of appeal and hold the appeal meeting.
6. Raise and deal with issues promptly, and act consistently.

The statutory right to be accompanied at disciplinary, grievance and appeal hearings is expressly included in the code — provided that the employee makes a "reasonable request". There is an obligation on employers (where previously it was just good practice) to advise employees of their right to be accompanied. Under the statutory right to be accompanied, all workers are entitled (when invited to attend any formal disciplinary interview or grievance hearing) to bring a "companion" of their choice to the meeting. The "companion" must be a fellow worker, a trade union representative or an official employed by a trade union. In 2015, Acas amended the code to clarify that, provided the chosen companion is one of these permitted categories of person, the employer must agree to the employee's choice — there is no provision entitling the employer to determine whether the choice of companion is reasonable. The code also states, however, that as a matter of good practice, the companion should be someone who is "suitable, willing and available on site".

The Disciplinary Regime Based on the Acas Code of Practice

Employment tribunals have the discretionary power to increase (or reduce) awards by up to 25% where the employer (or employee) has unreasonably failed to adhere to the relevant provisions of the Acas Code of Practice, *Disciplinary and Grievance Procedures*.

Grievance Procedures

The current regime is based on the principles set out in the Acas Code, *Disciplinary and Grievance Procedures*.

Keys to handling grievances

The Acas Code of Practice sets out the following "keys" to handling grievances in the workplace. The employee should:
- let the employer know the nature of the grievance.

On receipt of a grievance, the employer should:
- hold a meeting with the employee to discuss the grievance
- allow the employee to be accompanied at the meeting by a fellow worker or trade union representative of his or her choice
- decide on appropriate action
- allow the right of appeal.

Overlapping grievance and disciplinary cases

Where an employee raises a grievance during a disciplinary process, the disciplinary process may be temporarily suspended in order to deal with the grievance. Where the grievance and disciplinary cases are related, it may be appropriate to deal with both issues concurrently.

Collective grievances

The provisions of this Acas Code do not apply to grievances raised on behalf of two or more employees by a representative of a recognised trade union or other appropriate workplace representative. These grievances should be handled in accordance with the organisation's collective grievance procedure.

The Acas Code of Practice on Disciplinary and Grievance Procedures

The emphasis throughout the Acas Code of Practice on Disciplinary and Grievance Procedures, published in 2009 (and updated in March 2015), is on early resolution of workplace disputes and the code emphasises that many potential disciplinary problems or grievances can be resolved informally. Recourse to an employment tribunal should only be a last resort.

The code is supplemented and complemented by a more detailed but non-statutory Acas "good practice guidance" on handling disciplinary and grievance issues in the workplace, fleshing out the key points made in the code. The guidance encourages the use of external mediators to resolve disputes, provides advice on dealing with special issues such as absence and ill health, and suggests sample letters.

The Acas Code provides practical guidance to employers, employees and their representatives and sets out principles for handling disciplinary and grievance procedures in the workplace. The code:

- covers disciplinary action (including warnings) for misconduct or poor performance, but not redundancy, ill health dismissals or the expiry of fixed-term contracts
- encourages employers to consider mediation by third parties from either within or outside the organisation
- suggests that employees should be given copies of any written evidence, including witness statements, before a disciplinary hearing
- requires that employees be given a reasonable opportunity to present evidence and call witnesses at disciplinary hearings
- says that employers should involve employees and, where appropriate, their representatives in the development of disciplinary and grievance rules and procedures
- stresses the importance of ensuring managers and staff understand disciplinary and grievance rules and procedures, where they can be found and how they can be used
- requires employees to put their grievances in writing, to make every effort to attend meetings and to appeal disciplinary and grievance decisions if they disagree with them.

The code identifies the following principles — or "elements" — to be followed by employers if they are to deal fairly with such issues. These are as follows.

- Employers and employees should raise and deal with issues promptly and should not unreasonably delay meetings, decisions or confirmation of those decisions.
- Employers and employees should act consistently.
- Employers should carry out any necessary investigations, to establish the facts of the case.
- Employers should inform employees of the basis of the problem and give them an opportunity to put their case in response before any decisions are made.
- Employers should allow employees to be accompanied at any formal disciplinary or grievance meeting by a fellow worker or trade union representative of their choice.

Although the code is not legally binding, and a failure to follow any part of it does not make a person or organisation liable to proceedings, the employment tribunal will take it into account when assessing the fairness of any dismissal. An employer who has not followed the relevant provisions of the code should be prepared to explain why. The code sets out the basic requirements of fairness that are applicable in cases of discipline or when dealing with grievances.

A failure to follow the code
As explained above, a failure to follow the Acas Code does not give rise to a freestanding claim in the employment tribunal but an unreasonable failure to follow it by the employer or employee will entitle the tribunal, if it considers it just and equitable, taking into account the size and resources of the employer, to adjust the award by up to 25% either way.

Notice

An employee generally has the right to a period of notice, as set out in the contract of employment. This must not be less than the statutory minimum.

Minimum Periods of Statutory Notice

Length of continuous service	Period of notice
less than one month	none
1 month–2 years	one week
2–12 years	one week per year of service
12 or more years	12 weeks

The notice period may be dispensed with and no compensation offered in lieu if the employee commits an offence so serious that it is incompatible with continuing employment. This is known as *summary dismissal*.

If an employer dismisses an employee without notice, other than as a summary dismissal, the employer is obliged to pay the employee for the notice period. If this is allowed for in accordance with the contract of employment, the payment is subject to tax and National Insurance. If not, it will be regarded as compensation and may be free of tax and National Insurance, though advice should be sought from HMRC or a tax accountant.

Note: Proposals are in the pipeline to change the rules on the taxation of termination payments, specifically to make all pay-in-lieu of notice payments subject to income tax and Class 1 National Insurance contributions, regardless of whether or not the employee has a contractual entitlement to the payment.

Written Statement of Employment Particulars

All new employees (including full-time, part-time and temporary staff) whose employment continues for one month or more are entitled to a written statement explaining the principal terms and conditions of their employment. The statement (often, if inaccurately, referred to as the contract of employment) must be issued within two months of the date on which the employee began work (even if he or she resigns or is dismissed before the end of the two-month period). The statement of particulars does not constitute the contract of employment although it may be strong, but not conclusive, evidence of the terms of the contract. If both parties agree that the stated terms are correct (for example, by signing the statement to that effect), it will become a written contract. However, the statement will not become a contract of employment merely by the employee's acknowledgment of its receipt.

The statement must include the following particulars:
- the names of the employer and the employee
- the employee's job title or a brief description of the work
- date of commencement and date when period of continuous employment began
- amount of salary or wages, and when paid
- normal hours of work
- place of work
- details of any pension scheme

- terms and conditions regarding injury and sickness, including any provisions for sick pay
- period of notice (on both sides)
- entitlement to holidays and holiday pay (including bank and public holidays), and the method to be used to calculate entitlement, including accrued holiday pay on the termination of employment
- the length of employment, if not indefinite
- any collective agreements which affect the employment
- details of disciplinary and grievance procedures.

If the employee is to work overseas for more than one month, the written statement must also state:

- the period of work overseas
- the currency in which the employee will be paid
- any additional remuneration for working overseas
- any conditions relating to the employee's return to the UK.

If there are no particulars to be entered under any of the above items (eg if the employer does not operate an occupational sick pay or pensions scheme), the statement must say as much. A "Nil" return is unacceptable.

If any of the terms or conditions contained in the statement change, the employee must be informed in writing within one month.

Any employee who is not given a written statement or informed of any changes within the time limit, or who believes that his or her written statement is incorrect, may complain to an employment tribunal. Where no statement has been provided, the tribunal can determine which particulars it believes the parties agreed to and should have been written down. Where a statement has been provided but the employee is challenging its accuracy, the tribunal has the power to confirm, amend or substitute various particulars as it sees fit.

In cases where an employee is making another claim to the tribunal (eg unfair dismissal) and succeeds in that claim, an element of compensation may be awarded to reflect the employer's failure to provide a proper written statement. This will be either two or four weeks' pay (subject to the statutory limit on a week's pay).

Employment Protection Rights

Broadly speaking, all employees (and, in some instances, workers who are not employees) have the absolute or qualified right:

- not to be denied access to employment because of sex, being married or having a civil partner, gender reassignment, pregnancy, race, colour, nationality, national origins, ethnic origins, disability, sexual orientation, religion, belief or age, or on grounds of trade union membership (or non-membership), for failing to disclose details of a spent conviction

- to work in a safe and healthy working environment
- to be provided with as much information, instruction, training and supervision as is necessary to enable them to carry out their duties efficiently and safely
- to be issued with written statements explaining the principal terms and conditions of their employment (see above)
- to be issued with an itemised pay statement on each occasion they are paid
- to be paid at least the appropriate National Minimum Wage
- not to be required to work more than an average 48 hours a week (or, if under the age of 18, more than 40 hours a week or more than eight hours on any day)
- to the minimum daily, weekly and in-work rest breaks prescribed by the **Working Time Regulations 1998**
- to 28 days' paid holiday (or *pro rata* for part-time workers), which may include public or bank holidays
- not to suffer unauthorised deductions from their pay
- to be paid a guarantee payment if not provided with work on any day
- as protected or opted-out shop workers or betting workers, not to be dismissed or subjected to any other detriment for refusing to work on Sundays
- not to be dismissed or subjected to any detriment for making a protected disclosure
- not to be subjected to any detriment for carrying out (or proposing to carry out) their functions as trade union officials, workforce representatives, information and consultation representatives, members of a European Works Council, pension scheme trustees or safety representatives; or for applying for time off work for study or training; or for exercising their rights to maternity leave, adoption leave, paternity leave, shared parental leave or unpaid parental leave; or for applying for time off for dependants or for flexible working
- not to be dismissed or subjected to any detriment on the grounds that they are members of the reserve forces
- not to be dismissed or subjected to any detriment on the grounds that they have been summoned for, or have taken, time off work for jury service
- to be permitted a reasonable amount of paid time off work for study or training (young persons), for antenatal care or to attend pre-adoption

appointments; or to look for work (if under notice of redundancy); or to perform their duties as safety representatives, trade union officials, pension scheme trustees, or as employee or workforce representatives; or when accompanying a fellow employee or worker at the formal stages of a disciplinary or grievance procedure

- to be permitted a reasonable amount of unpaid time off work to carry out their activities as members of a recognised independent trade union or members of certain public bodies
- to maternity leave or adoption leave and (subject to service requirements) to paternity leave, shared parental leave or unpaid parental leave
- to request flexible working (subject to six months' continuous service)
- as part-time workers, not to be treated less favourably than comparable full-time workers working in the same establishment
- as fixed-term employees, not to be treated less favourably than comparable permanent employees working in the same establishment
- to be paid the same and to enjoy the same terms and conditions of employment as persons of the opposite sex doing the same or similar work, or work rated as equivalent or work of equal value
- not to be discriminated against on grounds of sex, race, disability, sexual orientation, trans-gender status, being married or a civil partner, pregnancy or maternity, religion, belief, trade union membership (or non-membership) or age
- not to be unfairly dismissed (subject to having had at least two years' continuous service) or dismissed for an inadmissible or unlawful reason
- not to be dismissed (or selected for redundancy) for asserting their statutory employment rights
- subject to having had at least two years' continuous service, to be paid redundancy pay when dismissed on grounds of redundancy, or if laid off work or kept on short-time working for four or more weeks (or for six or more weeks in the aggregate in any period of 13 consecutive weeks)
- to the protection afforded by the **Transfer of Undertakings (Protection of Employment) Regulations 2006**
- to be accompanied by a fellow worker or trade union representative of their choice at formal disciplinary and grievance meetings
- not to suffer detriment or dismissal in connection with making a request for "time off to train", (the right to request "time off to train" is limited to employees in organisations with 250+ employees)
- to apply to the Secretary of State for certain monies owed to them when their employer becomes insolvent

- to exercise rights relating to transnational information and consultation of employees
- to exercise rights in connection with the **Agency Workers Regulations 2010**.

Deductions from Wages

Only the following items may be deducted from wages:
- income tax and National Insurance
- student loan deductions
- attachment of earnings orders
- deductions specifically authorised by the employee in writing
- deductions authorised by a term of the employment contract, provided this has been notified in writing to the employee
- up to 10% of wages for deficiencies of stock or takings in the retail trade.

National Minimum Wage

Under the **National Minimum Wage Act 1998**, which is policed and enforced by HM Revenue & Customs (HMRC) inspectors, employers are duty-bound to pay the appropriate National Minimum Wage (NMW) to those of their workers who are aged 18 and over (a lower rate applies to 16- and 17-year-olds). The penalty for non-compliance is calculated as 200% (increased from 100% with effect from 1 April 2016) of the total underpayment for all the employees specified in the notice of underpayment. Where this amount would be less than £100, the minimum penalty of £100 will be applied. Where this amount would be more than £20,000, the maximum penalty of £20,000 should be applied. The penalty of up to £20,000 is payable in respect of each underpaid worker and is not the total fine payable by the employer (as was the case prior to 26 May 2015). The penalty is payable on top of the arrears of wages due to the affected worker(s). If the employer complies with the penalty notice within 14 days, the penalty stands to be reduced by 50%. In the most serious cases, employers can also face criminal prosecution.

Inspectors can also serve enforcement notices which require the employer to start paying the NMW and to make good any previous shortfall (including arrears to former employees who have left the company).

Current NMW rates

There are different levels of the NMW, depending on the individual's age and whether he or she is an apprentice. The rates as from 1 April 2018 are:

- £7.83 an hour for workers aged 25 and above
- £7.38 an hour for workers aged 21–24 inclusive
- £5.90 an hour for workers aged 18–20 inclusive
- £4.20 an hour for 16- and 17-year-olds
- £3.70 per hour for apprentices who are under age 19, or over age 19 but in the first year of their apprenticeship and employed under a contract of apprenticeship or engaged under certain Government arrangements.

As from 2017, the rates are reviewed in April each year, instead of in October as was previously the case.

The following do not qualify for the NMW: the genuinely self-employed, genuine volunteers, students doing work as part of their undergraduate or post-graduate course, workers on certain training schemes, residents of certain religious communities, prisoners, the armed forces and share fishermen.

However, there are no exemptions according to the size of business or by sector, job or region. All workers including pieceworkers, homeworkers, agency workers, commission workers, part-time workers and casual workers must receive at least the NMW.

The term "pay" for these purposes includes commission, bonus and performance-related pay, but does not include shift allowances, overtime premium payments, standby or "on call" payments, meal allowances or luncheon vouchers, "weighting" or cost of living allowances, clothing allowances, vehicle or travel allowances, deductions or payments in respect of protective clothing or equipment, medical insurance, or tips or gratuities (irrespective of how they are paid or distributed). Nor does it include that part of a deduction or payment in respect of live-in accommodation that currently exceeds £7.00 a day or £49.00 a week.

Workers who suspect that they are not being paid the correct NMW may write to their employers asking to see (and take copies of) their wage records. An employer who refuses or fails to produce those records within the following 14 days will be ordered by an employment tribunal to pay the worker in question an amount equal to 80 times the appropriate NMW, and to make good any underpayment of the NMW over whatever period the tribunal specifies. A worker has no need to resign in order to complain to an employment tribunal and will be awarded substantial compensation if dismissed or subjected to any other detriment for asserting his or her rights under the 1998 Act.

Employers must keep their payroll records on file for at least three years and must produce those records for inspection on demand by HMRC enforcement officers. The penalty for failing to maintain accurate and up-to-date records (or for failing to produce those records on demand) is an unlimited fine in the crown court. HMRC enforcement officers may also issue enforcement and penalty notices on employers. An enforcement notice will require the employer to start paying the NMW and to make good any previous shortfall. If the employer ignores the enforcement notice, the officer may serve a penalty notice which imposes a financial penalty calculated as a percentage of the total underpayment. This percentage figure increased from 50% to 100% and the figure for the maximum financial penalty increased from £5000 to £20,000 from 7 March 2014.

For further details, see *Reference Book for Employers*.

Discrimination

Equality Act 2010

On 1 October 2010, the main provisions of the **Equality Act 2010** came into force. This Act replaced (and repealed) all the previous discrimination laws which covered discrimination on grounds of sex, married status, civil partnership status, pregnancy/maternity, trans-gender status, race, disability, religion or belief, sexual orientation and age. The Equality Act largely re-enacted the provisions of the previous laws and also reconciled some of the differences between them. Some new provisions were also introduced.

The "protected characteristics"
The key principles governing equality at work apply across all the "strands" of discrimination (although there are also some specific provisions related to individual strands). The grounds on which discrimination is unlawful are now called "protected characteristics" these are:

- sex
- marriage and civil partnership status
- trans-gender status
- pregnancy/maternity
- race
- religion or belief
- sexual orientation
- age
- disability.

Types of Discrimination

Unlawful discrimination can take the form of direct discrimination, indirect discrimination, victimisation and harassment. In respect of disability, there is also discrimination "arising from disability" and a duty on the employer to make reasonable adjustments in respect of a disabled employee, worker or job applicant.

Where an adjustment involves a variation to the employee's contract of employment, such as a transfer to a different job or the removal of significant job responsibilities, the employer will only be able to legitimately implement the adjustment where the employee has consented to it. This was the ruling of the EAT in *G4S Cash Solutions (UK) Ltd v Powell* EAT 0243/15 who stated that where an employer seeks to make an adjustment that involves a variation of the employee's contract, the adjustment will not be effective unless the employee has agreed to the variation.

Direct discrimination

Direct discrimination occurs where an employee (or job applicant) is treated less favourably than someone else was or would be treated in similar circumstances and the reason for the less favourable treatment is one of the protected characteristics. Apart from direct age discrimination (which is open to justification), there is no possibility for an employer to justify direct discrimination unless an occupational requirement applies (see below).

Occupational requirements

It is lawful to discriminate on the grounds of one of the protected characteristics if an occupational requirement applies to a particular job (previously known as a genuine occupational requirement or GOR). This means that if the possession of a specified protected characteristic is a key element of the job in question (eg if there is a requirement for the job holder to be a man or a woman, to belong to a specified racial or religious group, to be heterosexual/gay/lesbian, to have a disability or to be in a particular age group), then it is lawful for the employer to discriminate against a job applicant or a candidate for promotion, transfer or training because he or she does not have that characteristic. For an occupational requirement to be lawful, the employer must also be able to show that its application in the particular case was proportionate when viewed in light of the need to achieve a defined legitimate aim.

The occupational requirement provisions are very narrow and operate as a limited exception to the general principles of equality in employment. An occupational requirement will be applicable only where there is a very clear connection between the work to be done and the characteristics required to perform it effectively.

Examples of occupational requirements could be where the employer seeks to employ a model to promote women's clothing, the employment of a gay person in a role that involves counselling gay couples, or the recruitment of someone from a specified racial group into a job that involves the provision of personal welfare services to people in a community where the members of the community are predominantly from that same racial group.

Discrimination by association and perception

The **Equality Act 2010** introduced two new concepts: discrimination by association and discrimination by perception.

Direct discrimination is unlawful irrespective of whether the protected characteristic that is the root cause of the discrimination is a characteristic of the complainant or of someone else. For example, if a white employee was instructed to discriminate against black people, that would amount to direct race discrimination against the white employee, even though it was not the white employee's race that was in issue. This is sometimes known as "discrimination by association".

Furthermore, discrimination that occurs because of a mistaken perception about an individual's protected characteristics is unlawful. For example, it would be unlawful to refuse to employ a particular job applicant because the person responsible for the decision as to whom to appoint mistakenly believed that he or she was gay. This is known as "discrimination by perception".

Indirect discrimination

Indirect discrimination is not as overt as direct discrimination; it can occur without an employer realising it and can sometimes be quite unintentional.

The **Equality Act 2010** defines indirect discrimination as occurring where an employer applies a "provision, criterion or practice (PCP)" to someone which is discriminatory in relation to a relevant protected characteristic and which:

- the employer applies, or would apply, to others with whom the individual does not share the characteristic
- puts, or would put, people with whom the individual shares the characteristic at a particular disadvantage when compared with people who do not share it
- puts, or would put, the individual at that disadvantage

- the employer cannot show to be a proportionate means of achieving a legitimate aim.

The phrase "provision, criterion or practice" has a broad meaning and would be likely to cover any policy, procedure, rule, requirement or condition applied by the employer, whether formally or informally. Indirect discrimination covers all the protected characteristics except pregnancy and maternity.

For example, an employer may set a number of different criteria which job applicants must satisfy in order to be considered for appointment to a particular vacant post. If the effect of one of these criteria is that women (or men), or people from a particular ethnic group, nationality, religion, sexual orientation or age or people with a particular disability are disadvantaged (ie they are less likely than others to be able to meet the particular criterion), then it will be indirectly discriminatory and, unless objectively justified, unlawful.

Take the case of a shorthand typist. If, for example, along with the speed requirements and other qualifications asked for, the employer added a requirement that applicants must be at least 5'10" tall, a woman who might otherwise be considered for the job could complain that the height criterion placed women at a disadvantage compared to men (because the average height of women is less than 5'10").

In order to remain within the law, the employer must be able to justify any provision, criterion or practice that is indirectly discriminatory. This will involve, first, showing that there was a legitimate business aim underpinning the application of the particular provision, criterion or practice (for example, the aim of ensuring competent performance of the job). Second, the application of the provision, criterion or practice must be proportionate, ie appropriate and necessary (and not excessive) in relation to the stated aim, eg necessary in order to ensure effective performance in the job.

To avoid unlawful indirect discrimination, an employer must be sure that all the selection criteria for a job can be justified as requirements of the job itself. Asking applicants to apply in writing for a purely manual vacancy, for instance, could be indirectly discriminatory against people of foreign nationality and also against those with certain types of disability, eg dyslexia.

Victimisation

A person may complain of being "victimised" under the **Equality Act 2010** if he or she has been penalised in some way because he or she has:

- brought discrimination proceedings against the employer
- given evidence or information in connection with proceedings brought by someone else
- made an allegation (whether or not express) that the employer has discriminated, for example, raised an internal grievance about alleged discriminatory treatment.

In practical terms, this means that employees and job applicants may complain to an employment tribunal of victimisation if they are unfavourably treated because they have previously complained of discriminatory treatment (whether through an internal grievance procedure or to an employment tribunal), given evidence or information in relation to a discrimination complaint or helped someone else to make a complaint.

Harassment

Behaviour will constitute harassment where it is "unwanted conduct related to a relevant protected characteristic", which has the purpose or effect of violating someone's dignity or creating an environment that is intimidating, hostile, degrading, humiliating or offensive for him or her.

Whether an individual's dignity has been violated or whether the conduct in question has created an uncomfortable or unpleasant working environment for him or her is largely subjective, ie it is up to each individual to decide for him- or herself what type of conduct is acceptable and what is offensive. The behaviour that is causing offence need not even be targeted at a particular individual — it will be enough if he or she is genuinely offended for a reason related to a relevant protected characteristic. For example, if an employee (of any race) persistently cracked racist jokes in an open-plan office and the jokes caused offence to a particular employee (again of any race), that could amount to racial harassment irrespective of whether the jokes were directed at any particular employee.

An important point to note is that the motive of the harasser is irrelevant; the key factor in determining whether behaviour amounts to harassment is the effect on the person at the receiving end.

Nevertheless, there is also a requirement that the behaviour must, in order to constitute unlawful harassment, be capable of being objectively viewed by a reasonable person as harassment.

Harassment perpetrated by third parties

The provision in the **Equality Act 2010** that made employers potentially vicariously liable for third-party harassment of employees has been abolished (with effect from 1 October 2013). This does not, however, mean that employers can never be held liable for the harassment of an employee perpetrated by a third party (eg a customer), as the main harassment provisions of the Act may be sufficient to create such liability.

Potential Claims

Claims to an employment tribunal are possible under the Equality Act from job applicants as well as existing employees. Claims are also possible from ex-employees where the discrimination is connected to their previous employment. For example, a claim could be brought against an employer who refused to provide an ex-employee with a reference because that employee, while employed, had brought a claim of discrimination against the employer to tribunal.

Claims can be brought not only by employees of the organisation, but also by apprentices and other "workers", eg contractors, casual workers and so on, provide they are required personally to do the work for the employer.

There is no minimum period of service required to bring a complaint of discrimination to an employment tribunal and no upper or lower age limit.

Employment Situations in which it is Unlawful to Discriminate

It is unlawful to discriminate in the following situations:
• recruitment and selection
• promotion
• transfer
• training
• the provision of benefits or facilities
• dismissal, including redundancy.

Recruitment

The **Equality Act 2010** makes it clear that there must be no discrimination at any stage of the recruitment process, including in the wording of advertisements, in the arrangements made for interviews, the interviews themselves and the decision as to whether or not to offer employment.

Examples of discriminatory arrangements for interviews could include asking a recruitment agency not to send black applicants or not to send women.

(Further information on recruitment is given at the start of the chapter.)

Positive Action

It is lawful in certain defined circumstances for an employer to take positive action by encouraging people with a defined protected characteristic (eg women or people from ethnic minority groups) to take up opportunities for employment or by offering them training that would help fit them for particular work. Positive action can be applied in respect of recruitment campaigns, advertising vacant posts and in training. Positive action is not mandatory and is permitted only in defined circumstances. The targeted group must, in the employer's reasonable view, be under-represented in the particular employment, or have different needs from those of people who do not share the same protected characteristic, or be disadvantaged because of the characteristic in question. The action taken must be aimed at reducing the under-representation, meeting the needs of people with the particular protected characteristic, or alleviating the disadvantage they have experienced. Additionally, the action taken by the employer must represent a proportionate way of addressing the particular under-representation, need or disadvantage.

To determine, for example, whether people of particular racial backgrounds are under-represented in the employment, the employer should consider first the extent to which the catchment area for recruitment contains a mixture of people of different races and nationalities. If so, the workforce should ideally contain the same mixture. For instance, if the place of work is situated in an area with a large Asian population but there are few Asian employees, the employer could take positive action by advertising the next vacancy in a publication that is read predominantly by Asian people. However, at the point of selection, the most suitable candidate must be chosen, regardless of race.

The concept of positive action is limited and voluntary and it is important to note that no employee or job applicant can lawfully be excluded from employment, promotion or training as a result of a positive action programme.

Recruitment campaigns
The type of action that would be permitted under this section would include (for example) aiming recruitment campaigns at people from minority ethnic groups or encouraging female employees to apply for promotion into management posts.

Advertising
Lawful positive action could include, for example, advertising vacancies in a publication read predominantly by women, or by younger (or older)

people. It would also be lawful to place an advertisement that openly encouraged members of minority ethnic groups to apply for a particular job, provided the advertisement also made it clear that selection would be carried out on merit without reference to race.

Training

It is also lawful, under the positive action provisions, to offer training to employees with a particular protected characteristic to help fit them for particular work. For example, an employer might offer computer training to employees aged over 50 or offer supervisory training to female employees in relatively junior positions to ensure that they had an equal opportunity for promotion along with their male colleagues.

Further positive action provisions

The Government brought an important provision of the **Equality Act 2010** into force from April 2011 allowing for further positive action measures to be taken in recruitment and promotion. In addition to the provisions described above, employers may, if they wish, apply further positive action measures at the point of selection for employment or promotion. Specifically, employers may choose to give preference to a candidate from an under-represented or disadvantaged group in circumstances where the candidate in question is at least "as qualified as" as another candidate. The phrase "as qualified as" is intended to refer not only to academic qualifications, but to all the criteria applicable to the post in question, eg relevant experience and skills. Any action taken must be a proportionate means of addressing the relevant under-representation or disadvantage.

This provision does not allow employers to apply a policy or practice of automatically treating people with a particular protected characteristic more favourably than others, even if this is done with a view to achieving equal representation in a particular part of the workplace.

Liability

Employers are liable for actions taken by their employees in the course of their employment, whether or not the employer was aware of the discriminatory act or approved of it. However, an employer that takes such steps as are reasonable to prevent an employee discriminating may be able to escape liability for a discriminatory act committed by an employee. Individual employees may also, at the tribunal's discretion, be held personally liable for their own acts of discrimination.

Tribunal Claims

An employee, worker, job applicant or ex-employee may bring a complaint of unlawful discrimination to an employment tribunal. Before submitting the claim, the employee must contact Acas with a view to early conciliation of the claim (although there is no positive duty on either the employee or the employer to engage in the conciliation process or agree to settle the claim). The claim must be lodged with the tribunal within three months of the alleged act of discrimination, but this time limit is put on hold during any period that the claim is with Acas. Ex-employees must bring a claim within three months of the act of discrimination, not within three months of the employment ending. The tribunal has discretion to extend the three-month time limit if it considers it just and equitable to do so, but exercises this discretion relatively rarely.

At the tribunal hearing, if the claimant proves facts from which the tribunal could conclude, in the absence of an adequate explanation, that discrimination has occurred, it will be for the employer to prove (on the balance of probabilities) either that discrimination did not occur or that its actions were lawful.

A tribunal has powers to make a declaration that there has been discrimination against the claimant, to recommend corrective action to be taken by the employer and/or to award compensation to the claimant. There is no financial ceiling on the amount of compensation that can be awarded to a successful complainant.

Any private settlement between the parties will be enforceable only if there has been conciliation by Acas or a settlement agreement in the required format.

The Equality and Human Rights Commission

From October 2007, the Equality and Human Rights Commission (EHRC), established under the **Equality Act 2006**, took over all the responsibilities and powers of the Equal Opportunities Commission, the Commission for Racial Equality and the Disability Rights Commission. The Commission (*www.equalityhumanrights.com*) has responsibility for the enforcement of the **Equality Act 2010**, as well as human rights legislation. The stated purpose of the EHRC is to "reduce inequality, eliminate discrimination, strengthen good relations between people and protect human rights".

The EHRC has produced two Codes of Practice related to employment law to accompany the **Equality Act 2010**; they cover employment and equal pay.

Default Retirement Age

The provisions in the **Equality Act 2010** which previously allowed employers to retire employees compulsorily at or above age 65 (the "default retirement age") without fear of age discrimination or unfair dismissal claims were abolished with effect from 6 April 2011.

It is still theoretically possible for individual employers to operate a compulsory retirement age, provided that they can objectively justify it. Objective justification means that the employer will, first, have to have a legitimate aim underpinning a policy of compulsory retirement at a specified age and, second, be able to show that applying that policy is appropriate and necessary with a view to achieving the stated aim.

Although a policy of compulsory retirement at a set age is, in theory, possible to justify, justification is likely to be very difficult in practice. This is because compulsory retirement amounts to direct age discrimination and the Supreme Court has ruled (in *Seldon v Clarkson Wright and Jakes* [2012] UKSC 16) that the legitimate aims relied on by the employer to justify direct age discrimination must be legitimate objectives of a public interest nature, such as employment policy, labour market objectives or the promotion of vocational training. They cannot be aims particular to the specific employer such as business efficiency. Furthermore, even if an employer can show that there is a legitimate aim of a public interest nature underpinning its policy of compulsory retirement, it also needs to be able to show that retiring employees at the selected age is appropriate and necessary in order to achieve that aim.

Time off Work

An employee is entitled to paid time off work for:

- antenatal care
- attendance at pre-adoption appointments (where the employee is proposing to adopt a child)
- certain duties and training as an official of a recognised independent trade union
- acting as a safety representative, or as an elected employee representative where there is no trade union representation
- looking for alternative work or retraining while under notice of redundancy, subject to qualifying service
- consultation with employers regarding redundancies and transfer of undertakings as part of his or her duties as a trade union appointed or employee-elected representative

- duties and training as an employee pension scheme trustee
- study or training by 16- and 17-year-olds
- accompanying a worker at a disciplinary or grievance hearing
- acting as a member of a European Works Council or as an information and consultation representative under the **Information and Consultation of Employees Regulations 2004**.

An employee is entitled to unpaid time off work for:

- the purpose of accompanying a pregnant spouse, partner or civil partner to up to two antenatal appointments
- the purpose of accompanying a spouse, partner or civil partner who is proposing to adopt a child to up to two pre-adoption appointments
- jury service
- sitting in court as a magistrate
- work as a member of a local authority
- work as a member of a statutory tribunal
- work as a governor of a school or college
- work as a member of a Scottish water and sewerage authority or a water industry consultative committee
- work as a member of a board of visitors for the prison authority
- work as a member of a police authority, appointed under the **Police Act 1996**
- work as a member of a National Health Service Trust or regional or area health authority or health board
- work as a member of the Service Authority for the National Criminal Intelligence Service or National Crime Squad
- work as a member of the Environment Agency or the Scottish Environment Protection Agency
- work as a member of the General Teaching Council for England or Wales
- certain activities as a member of a recognised independent trade union
- parental leave (subject to certain qualifying criteria)
- to deal with an emergency involving a dependant.

An employee has no statutory right to time off for:

- attending parliament or the European parliament
- campaigning for election to a local authority
- attending a church synod
- charity or voluntary work not otherwise included
- visits to doctor, dentist, optician, etc
- looking for alternative work when not under notice of redundancy
- training as a reserve in the armed forces.

Since 6 April 2010, employees in organisations with 250+ employees in Great Britain have had the right to request time off to train. The requests, which the employer has to consider, can lead to either qualifications for, or the acquisition of, new relevant skills.

Maternity Rights

A pregnant employee has the legal right:

- not to be dismissed, selected for redundancy or subjected to any other detriment because she is pregnant or for any reason connected with pregnancy or childbirth
- to be permitted a reasonable amount of paid time off work for antenatal care (as advised by her doctor or registered midwife)
- to take up to 52 weeks' maternity leave, comprising 26 weeks' ordinary maternity leave (OML), followed by up to 26 weeks' additional maternity leave (AML)
- to switch from maternity leave to "shared parental leave" provided the employee and her partner both have at least 26 weeks' continuous service
- to return to work in the same job (or, in prescribed circumstances, to a suitable alternative job) after maternity leave
- to be paid up to 39 weeks' statutory maternity pay (SMP) during her maternity pay period, provided her average weekly earnings are at or above the "lower earnings limit" for NICs purposes (£116 a week from April 2018), and provided she has been continuously employed for 26 or more weeks by the end of the 15th week before her expected week of childbirth (EWC); payment is at 90% of average weekly earnings for the first six weeks and thereafter at the standard weekly rate, currently £145.18 per week
- to be issued with a written statement explaining the reasons for her dismissal if dismissed while pregnant or during her ordinary or additional maternity leave periods
- to be paid her normal wages or salary if suspended from work on maternity grounds (unless she has unreasonably refused an offer of suitable alternative employment)
- to be transferred from night work to day work if, in the opinion of her doctor, her employment at night is detrimental to her health or that of her child or developing foetus
- to have access to suitable rest facilities during normal working hours (such facilities to be provided by her employer under regulation 25(4) of the **Workplace (Health, Safety and Welfare) Regulations 1992**)

- a woman undergoing IVF treatment will be regarded as pregnant following the implantation of the fertilised ova.

Note: Protection against discrimination lasts from the beginning of pregnancy through to the end of the employee's maternity leave (known as the "protected period").

There is no need for any form of comparator in pregnancy or maternity-related discrimination claims.

Maternity Leave

As already indicated, all pregnant employees, subject to giving the correct notice to the employer, have a legal right of up to 52 weeks' maternity leave. The first period of 26 weeks of this leave is called "ordinary maternity leave"; the second period of 26 weeks is known as "additional maternity leave". There is no qualification period for the right to the period of additional maternity leave.

All the employee's contractual rights, apart from remuneration, continue during the whole of the maternity leave period. These include the following.

- Benefits such as a company car, medical insurance, etc.
- The accrual of contractual and statutory holiday under the working time regulations.
- Seniority and similar rights.

Note: The Government introduced a system of shared parental leave in respect of parents whose child was due to be born on or after 5 April 2015. Under the scheme, mothers can choose to bring their maternity leave to an end on a specified date and share the untaken balance of the leave with their husband, partner, civil partner or the father of the child. Shared parental leave gives parents much more flexibility than they have under maternity legislation as they can choose to share up to 50 weeks of leave between them either concurrently or separately and either in continuous or discontinuous blocks. Shared parental leave is discussed later in this chapter.

Qualification and Notification

Every pregnant employee has the legal right to take up to 52 weeks' maternity leave. To qualify, she must notify her employer, by the end of the 15th week before her EWC, of the date on which she intends her ordinary maternity leave to start (and, if asked to do so, must produce for her employer a certificate of expected confinement (Form Mat B1) signed by her doctor or registered midwife). Her employer must respond in writing, within the next 28 days, informing her of the date on which she is expected to return to work if she takes her full entitlement of maternity leave. Failure by the employer to do this could prejudice its right to take action against the employee for returning to work unexpectedly early or for failing to return on time.

A pregnant employee may change her mind about the intended start date, so long as she informs her employer at least 28 days before the new date or original date, whichever comes first. The following points should also be noted.

- Unless she gives birth prematurely, an employee may not begin her ordinary maternity leave before the beginning of the 11th week before her EWC.
- A pregnant employee incapacitated with a pregnancy-related illness, at any time after the beginning of the fourth week before her EWC, must begin her maternity leave on the day on which that incapacity occurred.

Rights on Return to Work

An employee may return to work before the end of her maternity leave if she gives her employer at least eight weeks' notice of the date on which she intends to return to work. However, she may not return to work within two weeks of giving birth (or within four weeks of that date if she works in a factory).

An employee made redundant during her maternity leave period has the right — in preference to any other redundant employees — to be offered any suitable alternative vacancy under a new contract of employment that begins on the day immediately following the day on which her employment under her previous contract came to an end. This right applies irrespective of how many weeks or months' maternity leave the employee still has left.

An employee who returns to work at or before the end of her ordinary maternity leave has the right to return to work with her employer in the job she occupied immediately before her ordinary maternity leave began.

An employee who returns to work during or at the end of her additional maternity leave is entitled either to return to the job she held before the start of her maternity leave, or, if this is not reasonably practicable, to be offered another job which is suitable and appropriate for her to do, and is on terms that are no less favourable. Failure to take back an employee at the end of her maternity leave will constitute unfair dismissal and probably sex discrimination.

Note: If there has been an annual shutdown for the purposes of statutory annual leave during the employee's maternity leave, she will be entitled to take an equivalent period of holiday at another time after she has returned to work.

Parental Leave

Under the **Maternity and Parental Leave Regulations 1999**, employees who have been with their employer for at least one year and who have, or expect to have, parental responsibility for a child have the legal right to take up to 18 weeks' unpaid parental leave. This was increased from 13 weeks to 18 weeks in March 2013.

As from 5 April 2015, the right to take parental leave lasts up until the child's 18th birthday.

To qualify for parental leave, as well as having at least one year's service with his or her current employer, the employee must:

• be the parent (named on the birth certificate) of a child who is under age 18

• have acquired (or expect to acquire) formal parental responsibility for the child

• have adopted a child under the age of 18.

In the absence of any "in-house" procedures for the taking of parental leave (or any term in a collective or workforce agreement concerning such leave), the "fallback" scheme outlined in schedule 2 to the 1999 Regulations comes into play. Under that scheme (which appears to have been adopted by most employers), an eligible employee may take up to four weeks' parental leave in any one year (but only in tranches of one week or more).

Furthermore, an employee seeking to take parental leave must submit his or her request at least 21 days before the date on which that period of leave is intended to begin and must, if asked to do so, produce evidence of parental responsibility. The employer may postpone the requested period of leave for up to six months (suggesting an alternative start date) if the employee's absence is likely to do serious harm to the employer's business. However, postponement is not permissible if an employee's requested period of parental leave is intended to begin on the day of a child's birth or its placement with its new parents for adoption.

An employee who takes parental leave for four weeks or less is entitled to return to work in the job he or she occupied before that period of leave began. An employee who takes more than four weeks' parental leave at any one time may likewise return to work in the same job or, if it is not reasonably practicable for the employer to permit the employee to return to that job, to another job that is both suitable for the employee and appropriate for him or her to do in the circumstances.

For further information, see *Reference Book for Employers*.

Adoption Leave

Under the Paternity and Adoption Leave Regulations, eligible employees (whether male or female, and whether married, single or civil partners) are entitled to take adoption leave when they adopt a child. Where a couple adopts a child jointly, one may take adoption leave and the other paternity leave (subject to the qualifying conditions). It is up to them to decide which of them takes which.

As from 5 April 2015, adoption leave is available to prospective parents who take part in the "fostering for adoption" scheme and also to intended parents in a surrogacy arrangement (provided they meet the normal eligibility conditions).

Additionally, as from 5 April 2015, there is no length of service required for an employee to be eligible for adoption leave. Prior to that date, an employee had to have at least 26 weeks' continuous service with the employer (calculated at the end of the week in which the employee was notified of the match with the child).

The entitlement is to take up to 52 weeks' adoption leave, comprising 26 weeks' ordinary adoption leave followed by 26 weeks' additional adoption leave. Employees with average weekly earnings equal to or greater than the lower earnings limit (LEL) for NICs (currently £116 per week) who have been continuously employed by their respective employers for 26 or more weeks by the end of the week in which they received formal notification of having been matched with a child, will also qualify for statutory adoption pay (SAP) during their adoption leave periods.

Note: The Government has introduced a new system of shared parental leave in respect of parents whose child was due to be born or placed for adoption on or after 5 April 2015. Under the shared parental leave scheme, adopters can choose to bring their adoption leave to an end on a specified date and share the untaken balance of the leave with their spouse, partner, civil partner or the father of the child.

Shared parental leave gives parents much more flexibility than they have under adoption/paternity legislation as they can choose to share up to 52 weeks of leave between them either concurrently or separately and either in continuous or discontinuous blocks. Shared parental leave is discussed later in this chapter.

To exercise their right to adoption leave, employees must inform their employers of their intention to take such leave within seven days of having been notified by their adoption agency that they have been matched with a child for adoption. If asked to do so, they must also provide the appropriate documentary evidence (the "matching certificate" issued by the adoption agency can be used for this purpose).

Employees can choose to start their adoption leave from the date of the child's placement with them (whether this is earlier or later than expected) or from a fixed date which can be up to 14 days before the expected date of placement. Employees who have correctly notified their employers of the date on which they intend to start their adoption leave may change their minds, so long as they inform their employers of that change of mind at least 28 days before the new start date or the original date, whichever occurs first.

An employer, who has been correctly notified of the date on which an eligible employee intends to start his or her adoption leave, must write to the employee in question, within the next 28 days, setting out the date on which the employee would be expected to return to work if his or her full entitlement to adoption leave is taken.

All the employee's contractual rights, apart from remuneration, continue as normal throughout adoption leave.

Statutory Adoption Pay

An employee who qualifies for adoption leave, and who has average weekly earnings equal to or greater than the lower earnings limit for NIC purposes (currently £116) will normally qualify for up to 39 weeks' statutory adoption pay. SAP is paid to eligible employees for the first six weeks of adoption leave at the rate of 90% of the employee's average weekly earnings (as is the case for statutory maternity pay). Thereafter, SAP is payable for up to 33 weeks at the flat rate of £145.18 per week (as from April 2018) or 90% of the employee's average weekly earnings, whichever is the lower of those amounts. Prior to 5 April 2015, SAP was paid at the flat weekly rate throughout the full adoption pay period.

An employer who has lawfully paid SAP to an employee may claim back 92% of the amount paid by deducting the amount in question from the payments of employees' and employers' NICs made to the Collector of Taxes at the end of each tax month. Employers who are eligible for small employers' relief may recover 100% of the amount of SAP paid, plus an additional amount in compensation (currently 3%) for the employer's portion of NICs paid on SAP.

Further Information

For further information on adoption leave and pay, see *Reference Book for Employers*.

Paternity Leave

The right to take paternity leave was first introduced under the **Paternity and Adoption Leave Regulations 2002**. The initial right was to a period of two weeks' paternity leave following the birth or adoption of a child (see below). The right was extended in April 2011 with the introduction of "additional paternity leave" (under the **Work and Families Act 2006**) but this was subsequently phased out and replaced with "shared parental leave" (see below).

Note: Under the shared parental leave scheme, employees can choose to bring their maternity or adoption leave to an end on a specified date and share the untaken balance of the leave with their spouse, partner, civil partner or the father of the child. Shared parental leave gives parents much more flexibility than they have under maternity/paternity or adoption legislation as they can choose to share up to 52 weeks of leave between them either concurrently or separately and either in continuous or discontinuous blocks. Shared parental leave is discussed later in this chapter.

To qualify for paternity leave, an employee must:

- have been continuously employed by his or her employer for a period of 26 weeks or more by the end of the 15th week before the mother's EWC or by the end of the week in which the child's adopter is notified of having been matched with the child for adoption
- be the child's father and/or the mother's husband or partner (including same-sex partners, whether or not this is a civil partnership) or (in an adoption situation) be married to, or the partner of, the child's adopter
- have or expect to have the main (albeit shared) responsibility for the child's upbringing.

Entitlement to Paternity Leave

Employees who qualify have the right to take either one week's paternity leave or two consecutive weeks' leave within 56 days of the child's date of birth. The same right extends to employees (of either sex) whose spouse or partner has a child placed with them for adoption.

Eligible employees who wish to exercise their right to paternity leave must notify their employers (in writing) by the end of the 15th week before the EWC.

Most employees will be entitled to statutory paternity pay (SPP) during their absences from work on paternity leave.

Completing and submitting HMRC Form SC3 (*Becoming a Parent*) will satisfy the notification requirements for both paternity leave and SPP. Where paternity leave is taken in cases of adoption, the employee must notify the employer within seven days of being notified by the adoption agency that there has been a match with a child. This may be done on HMRC form SC4 (*Becoming an Adoptive Parent*).

Return to Work After Paternity Leave

An employee returning to work after paternity leave has the legal right to do so in the job he or she occupied immediately before that period of leave began, without any loss of seniority or pension rights, or any other rights dependent on a period of employment.

Statutory Paternity Pay

An eligible employee will qualify for SPP during his or her absence from work on paternity leave if he or she has average weekly earnings equal to or greater than the current LEL for NIC purposes. For 2018/19, the LEL is £116 per week. SPP is payable at the same standard rate as SMP, ie £145.18 a week from April 2018, or 90% of the employee's average weekly earnings at the time, whichever is the lower of those amounts.

Employers who have lawfully paid SPP to an employer are (as is the case with payments of SMP) able to recover an amount equal to 92% of the amount paid by deducting it from PAYE tax and NICs routinely remitted to HMRC at the end of each income tax month. Small employers (the total of whose NICs did not exceed £45,000 during the preceding tax year) will, on the other hand, be able to recover 100% of the amount of SPP paid, plus a further 3% to recoup the additional NICs paid on such payments.

Further Information

Forms SC3 and SC4 are available from the Employer's Orderline on 0845 7 646 646.

See *Reference Book for Employers.*

Shared Parental Leave

As discussed elsewhere in this book, employees who give birth to a child have a legal right to take up to 52 weeks' maternity leave subject to their complying with certain notification requirements. Parallel rights are available to employees who adopt a child.

In addition to these rights, there is a right to "shared parental leave" subject to certain conditions, restrictions and notice requirements. Under the shared parental leave provisions, eligible employees have the choice to bring their maternity leave to an end, enabling them to share the untaken balance of the leave with their husband, partner, civil partner or the father of the child. Parallel provisions apply to employees who are entitled to adoption leave.

As is the case during maternity and adoption leave, all the employee's contractual rights, apart from remuneration, continue in force during shared parental leave. These include the following.

- Benefits such as a company car, medical insurance, etc.
- The accrual of statutory holiday under the Working Time Regulations.
- Seniority and similar rights.

Eligibility for Shared Parental Leave

To be eligible for shared parental leave, an employee must have at least 26 weeks' continuous service with the employer, calculated (for pregnant employees) at the end of the 15th week before the EWC or (for employees adopting a child) at the end of the week in which the employee was notified of the match with the child. This is termed the "relevant date".

An additional condition for the employee to be eligible is that his or her spouse or partner must satisfy the "employment and earnings test" which requires the spouse or partner to have been an employed or self-employed earner in Britain for a minimum of 26 weeks (which can be continuous or discontinuous) during the 66 weeks leading up to the EWC or adoption placement. Additionally, he or she must have earned an average of at least £30 per week during 13 of those weeks.

For the employee's spouse or partner (or the father of the child) to be eligible to take shared parental leave, he or she must have at least

26 weeks' continuous service as at the "relevant date". He or she must also expect to have responsibility for the care of the child, must remain in continuous employment until the week before he or she starts shared parental leave and must comply with defined notification requirements (see below).

Shared parental leave may be taken at any time from the date on which the child is born or placed for adoption. For employees who give birth, however, it cannot begin until the start of the third week after the date of the child's birth. All periods of shared parental leave must be completed by the day before the child's first birthday or the first anniversary of the date of the adoption placement. Shared parental leave must be taken in complete weeks and the minimum period of leave that an employee can take is one week. Shared parental leave can, however, start on any day of the week.

Notice Requirements

To exercise their right to shared parental leave, employees must fulfil certain notice requirements. First, the employee who is switching to shared parental leave from maternity or adoption leave must give his or her employer a written "curtailment notice", the purpose of which is simply to bring the maternity or adoption leave period to an end on a specified date and allow the untaken balance to be taken as shared parental leave instead.

Next, both the employee and his or her spouse or partner are each required to submit a "notice of entitlement" to their respective employers. The intention of the notice of entitlement is simply to give the employer an indication of the periods of leave that the employee is considering. The notice of entitlement must be accompanied by a declaration from the employee and one from the spouse or partner confirming their eligibility for shared parental leave and providing certain information.

Both the curtailment notice and the notice of entitlement must be given at least eight weeks before the start date of the first period of shared parental leave that the employee (or the spouse or partner) proposes to take.

Third, the employee (and his or her spouse or partner) must submit "booking notices" to their respective employers for each period of shared parental leave that they wish to take, giving at least eight weeks' notice and setting out the intended start and end dates of the leave period(s) requested. The first booking notice can be provided at the same time as, or after, the employee's "notice of entitlement" is lodged, but not before.

A booking notice can request either a single continuous period of shared parental leave or two or more discontinuous blocks of leave, ie a request for two or more separate periods of leave interspersed with periods when the employee returns to work.

Both the employee and his or her spouse or partner are entitled to give three notices to book three separate periods of shared parental leave, ie the original notification plus two further notifications or changes to pre-notified dates. Consequently, the employer cannot refuse the employee's first three requests for continuous periods of shared parental leave provided the notice provisions have been properly complied with.

An employer has the right, however, to refuse to grant a request for discontinuous blocks of shared parental leave. Following such a request, the employer and employee have a period of two weeks to discuss the pattern of leave requested. The employer may then agree to the request, propose an alternative pattern of leave, or refuse the request.

Where a request for discontinuous leave is refused (or where no agreement is reached after two weeks), the employee is entitled by default to take the total block of leave covered in the booking notice as one continuous period. Alternatively, the employee may withdraw the booking notice (so long as he or she does so on or before the 15th day after the date on which the booking notice was originally submitted). The employee may subsequently submit a new request for a continuous block of leave or a different pattern of discontinuous leave.

Note: This type of withdrawal notice does not count towards the limit of three booking/variation notices that the employee is entitled to submit.

Statutory Shared Parental Pay

Employees with average weekly earnings equal to or greater than the LEL for NICs (currently £116 per week) may also be eligible to share up to 39 weeks of ShPP with their spouse, partner, civil partner or the father of the child. To be eligible for ShPP, the employee must also have been continuously employed for 26 or more weeks by the end of the 15th week before the EWC or (for adoptive parents) by the end of the week in which formal notification of a match with a child was received.

Further eligibility conditions are that the employee (and his or her spouse or partner) must be absent from work and must propose to care for the child during each week in respect of which SSPP is paid. The spouse or partner must also satisfy the "employment and earnings" test (see above).

The employee and the spouse or partner must each submit certain notices to their respective employers in order to activate ShPP. The employee who was entitled to SMP or SAP must first submit a "pay curtailment notice" in writing specifying the date on which he or she wants to bring maternity or adoption pay to end. The employee must give a minimum of eight weeks' notice of this date.

Thereafter, both the employee and his or her spouse or partner must submit notices to their respective employers to claim SSPP. These notices must also be given at least eight weeks in advance of the date on which the employee wishes ShPP to start. Detailed information about entitlement to ShPP and the amounts that each partner intends to claim must be included within the notice.

Unlike SMP, there is just one standard rate of ShPP, which is £145.18 a week (from April 2018), or 90% of the employee's average weekly earnings, whichever is the lower of those amounts.

An employer who has lawfully paid ShPP to an employee may claim back 92% of the amounts paid by deducting the amounts in question from the payments of employees' and employers' NICs made to the Collector of Taxes at the end of each tax month. Employers who are eligible for small employers' relief may recover 100% of the amount of ShPP paid, plus an additional amount in compensation (currently 3%) for the employer's portion of NICs paid on ShPP.

Rights on Return to Work

Employees have the right to return to the same job after any period of maternity, paternity, adoption or shared parental leave totalling 26 weeks or less in aggregate, even if the leave is taken in discontinuous blocks. This right is unaffected if the employee takes a period of up to four weeks' unpaid parental leave as well.

Where, however, an employee returns to work following a period of more than 26 weeks' leave (in aggregate), or after a period of up to 26 weeks' leave combined with a period of unpaid parental leave of more than four weeks, the right to return is either to the same job or (if that is not reasonably practicable) to another job which is suitable and appropriate for him or her to do and is on terms (including pay) that are no less favourable.

A failure or refusal to take back an employee at the end of shared parental leave will constitute an unfair dismissal.

Right to Request Time Off for Training

From April 2010, there is a provision allowing employees of all ages, subject to their having a minimum of six months' service, to request time off work to train. The right applies only to employees who work for an employer with 250 or more staff.

This right is to ask for time off, not to be given it on demand.

In order for a request for time off to train to be valid, the study or training for which the employee requests time off must be of a type which will help him or her to be more effective at work, and which is either an accredited programme leading to a qualification, or unaccredited training which will help him or her develop a specific skill relevant to his or her job. Additionally, the training must be of a type that will help the employer improve its business performance.

Once an employer has received a valid request from an eligible employee, it is under a duty to follow through a set procedure to consider it. The mandatory procedure requires the employer to:

- hold a meeting with the employee to discuss the application within 28 days of receiving the request
- permit the employee to be accompanied at the meeting by a colleague of his or her choice
- provide a written response to the employee within 14 days of the meeting which must either agree to the employee's request or refuse it, in which case the employer must state the grounds on which the refusal is based
- provide details of the appeal process to the employee if the request has been refused.

An employer may only refuse a valid request for time off for study or training if the refusal is for one of the business reasons provided for in the legislation. These reasons mirror those applicable to requests for flexible working which are refused. The permissible grounds for refusal are:

- the burden of additional costs
- detrimental effect on the ability to meet customer demand
- inability to re-organise work among existing staff
- inability to recruit additional staff
- detrimental impact on quality
- detrimental impact on performance
- insufficiency of work during the periods the employee proposes to work
- planned structural changes.

The employer may also refuse a request if it thinks that the proposed study or training would not improve the employee's effectiveness in the business or the performance of the business itself.

Employers are not obliged to pay the employee for any time off granted for this purpose, nor are they obliged to organise or pay for the study or training.

For more information see *Reference Book for Employers*.

Flexible Working

As from 30 June 2014, the right to request flexible working — such as a shorter working week, a system of staggered or annualised hours, flexi-time, job sharing, part-time work, term-time working, self-rostering, working from home and so on — is available to *all* employees (whether male or female) provided they have at least 26 weeks' service. Prior to this date, the right was available only to employees who had parental responsibility for a child under the age of 17 or caring responsibilities for a dependant adult.

One remaining restriction is that, in order to be eligible to submit a request, the employee must not have submitted an earlier application for flexible working within the previous 12 months.

Although employees have no legal right to demand more flexible working arrangements, their employers are duty-bound both to consider seriously any such application and to explain their reasons if they feel that they are unable to accommodate the employee's desired new work pattern.

The relevant legislation is to be found in ss.80F–80I of the **Employment Rights Act 1996** and the **Children and Families Act 2014**.

Employer's Response

The previous mandatory procedure for dealing with requests for flexible working was abolished with effect from 30 June 2014. In its place is a simple requirement that employers must deal with applications for flexible working "in a reasonable manner". Another requirement is that the employer must notify the employee of its decision within three months of the application (unless an extension of time is agreed with the employee). The employer should also:

- specify the contract variation that has been agreed and the date on which it is to take effect (if the request is agreed or an appeal upheld)
- set out the grounds on which the refusal is based (if the request, or the appeal, has been refused).

The provisions in the original legislation allowing employers the right to refuse a request for flexible working on certain business grounds have been retained (see next section).

Acas has published a statutory Code of Practice which sets out the principles that employers should follow when dealing with requests for flexible working. The code states that employers should:

- arrange to talk to the employee as soon as possible after receiving a written request for flexible working (unless the intention is to approve the request straight away)
- adopt the approach that requests will be granted unless there is a business reason for not granting a particular request
- discuss the employee's request directly with him or her, where possible in private
- allow the employee to be accompanied by a colleague at any discussion about flexible working
- inform the employee of the decision in writing as soon as possible
- if the employee's request is granted, discuss with him or her when and how the changes might best be implemented
- if the employee's request is rejected, ensure that the rejection is for one of the business reasons permitted by legislation and allow the employee to appeal the decision.

Acas has produced a separate non-statutory guide that provides good practice guidance for employers.

Grounds for Refusing an Application for Flexible Working

Employers may only refuse an application for flexible working if one or more of the following business reasons applies:
(a) the burden of additional costs
(b) detrimental effect on the ability to meet customer demand
(c) inability to re-organise work among existing staff
(d) inability to recruit additional staff
(e) detrimental impact on quality or performance
(f) insufficiency of work during the periods the employee proposes to work
(g) planned structural changes.

Complaints

An employee may refer the matter to an employment tribunal if the employer:
- provides a false or non-valid reason for refusing his or her request

- rejects the application on grounds other than those listed above
- bases the decision on inaccurate facts.

Alternatively, and with the employer's agreement, the employee may refer the issue to binding arbitration by an Acas-appointed independent arbitrator (under the Acas Arbitration Scheme).

Should an employment tribunal uphold any such complaint, it will make a declaration to that effect and may order the employer either to reconsider the employee's application and/or pay such compensation to the employee as it considers to be just and equitable in the circumstances (subject to a maximum of eight weeks' pay).

Further Information

See *Reference Book for Employers* and *Personnel in Practice — Records and Procedures*.

Agency Workers

Employment agencies and businesses which supply employers with workers are governed by the **Employment Agencies Act 1973** and the **Conduct of Employment Agencies and Employment Businesses Regulations 2003**. Most of the provisions came into force on 6 April 2004. The legislation covers both employment agencies, which introduce workers to employers, and employment businesses, which hire out their own employees to other employers — usually on a temporary basis.

The main provisions are as follows.

- Before supplying services to a workseeker, agencies and employment businesses are required to obtain their agreement to basic terms, including details of any fees. Terms of agreement must also be reached with the hirer before they are provided with services.
- Where agencies supply staff to work with vulnerable groups such as children, the elderly or the infirm, they are required to carry out checks. These include obtaining copies of relevant qualifications, obtaining two references and taking all reasonable steps to confirm that an individual is not unsuitable. Furthermore, if new, adverse information subsequently comes to light, the agency must withdraw the worker or, in cases where the worker has been supplied on a permanent basis, inform the employer. The same rules apply where the worker is required by law, or by any professional body, to have any qualification or authorisation to work in the position concerned.

- Employment businesses are not entitled to withhold workers' pay purely because they cannot produce an authenticated timesheet.
- Agencies must obtain information on any health and safety risks known to the hirer and the steps taken to prevent or control those risks.
- Agencies placing actors, models and other entertainers are not allowed to charge upfront fees before they find them work.
- The use of "temp to perm" fees — which agencies charge when temporary workers take up permanent jobs with the hirer — is limited. The regulations impose a maximum quarantine period of 14 weeks from the start of an assignment (or eight weeks after it finishes, whichever comes later) that must pass before the employer can take the worker on permanently without having to pay a fee.

The Employment Agency Standards Inspectorate enforces the **Employment Agencies Act 1973** and its associated regulations (as above). It can prosecute agencies and employment businesses for breaching the legislation and impose a fine of up to £5000 for each offence. It can also apply to an employment tribunal for a prohibition order which can prohibit a person from operating an agency for up to 10 years.

Employment Status of Agency Workers

There are an estimated 1.4 million agency workers in the UK. These workers are frequently hired by employers from employment businesses ("agencies"). In a typical "triangular" relationship, the agency engages the services of an individual to work for another (the "end-user"). The employment status of these agency workers has consistently caused particular legal problems.

The position was clarified in *James v London Borough of Greenwich* in which the Court of Appeal set down the following principles.

- The issue relating to the status of atypical workers engaged in the triangular relationship is a question of fact to be decided by the employment judge in accordance with the common law principles of implied contract.
- As long as the arrangements between the three parties are genuine, there is no need to imply a contract between the end-user and the worker, even if such a contract would not be inconsistent with the relationship between them.
- It will be unusual (rare) for a tribunal to imply such a contract — only where the agency arrangements are a sham or the worker has previously been an employee of the end-user; indeed, the Court of

Appeal said that an appellate court should only review the decision if there is a clear error of law.

- Neither the "mere passage of time" (ie the length of service with the end-user) nor the extent to which the worker is integrated into the employer's organisation is decisive in determining an implied contract.

In the light of this decision, it is difficult for an agency worker to claim and secure employee status with the hiring organisation.

Agency Workers' Regulations

In October 2011, the **Agency Workers Regulations 2010** came into force. The regulations implement the EU Directive on Temporary Agency Work and provide the following rights for temporary agency workers.

- Equal treatment for temporary agency workers compared to comparable permanent workers engaged in the same organisation after 12 calendar weeks' working in that organisation in the same role.
- Equal access from day one of their assignments to collective facilities such as staff canteens, childcare facilities and transport services.
- Equal right to information about any relevant permanent job vacancies within the hirer's organisation from the first day of their assignments.

The EAT has confirmed (in *Moran and ors v Ideal Cleaning Services Ltd and anor* [2013] EAT 0274/13) that agency workers supplied to a client on an indefinite (or permanent) basis do not fall within the scope of the regulations.

The right to equal treatment applies only in respect of certain basic working and employment conditions, namely basic pay, overtime payments, allowances for working shifts or unsocial hours, commission, bonuses based on personal performance, vouchers or stamps which have monetary value, working time, rest periods and rest breaks, night work, and entitlement to holidays and holiday pay.

Occupational sick pay, redundancy pay, maternity/paternity/adoption rights and non-cash benefits (eg private medical insurance) and access to profit sharing schemes and pension schemes are not covered.

The regulations contain anti-avoidance measures that are intended to prevent employers from avoiding giving agency workers the rights to which they are entitled by engaging them on a series of assignments each lasting less than 12 weeks.

The regulations do not impact on the employment status of agency workers.

Rehabilitation of Offenders

Generally, a person convicted of a minor offence does not have to disclose that conviction to a prospective employer after a rehabilitation period.

Rehabilitation periods vary depending on the type and length of conviction originally incurred.

With effect from 10 March 2014, amendments were made to the **Rehabilitation of Offenders Act 1974**. The periods of time needed for convictions to become "spent" were reduced and (for custodial sentences) now consist of the period of the sentence, plus an additional specified period, known as a "buffer period".

Rehabilitation Periods

Sentence length	Rehabilitation period
0–6 months	Period of sentence plus 2 years
6–30 months	Period of sentence plus 4 years
30 months–4 years	Period of sentence plus 7 years
More than 4 years	Can never become spent

Non-custodial sentences	Rehabilitation period
Community order or youth rehabilitation order	1 year from end of sentence
Fine	1 year from date of conviction
Absolute discharge	None (previously 6 months)
Conditional discharge, referral order, reparation order, action plan order, supervision order, bind-over order, hospital order	Period of order

For the following occupations, even minor offences never become "spent":

- solicitors, barristers, judges, coroners and other lawyers
- accountants
- medical staff (doctors, surgeons, nurses, physiotherapists, dentists, veterinary surgeons, etc)
- those employed by courts or the probation service
- police officers
- teachers
- operators of the national lottery

- those in jobs or positions which give them access to vulnerable adults
- those in jobs which involve working with people under the age of 18.

Checks on Job Applicants

The Criminal Records Bureau (CRB) was created under the provisions of the **Police Act 1997** to enable employers to ask prospective employees or volunteers to apply for a criminal record check. The Bureau is now called the Disclosure and Barring Service (DBS). The DBS can issue three different types of certificate each representing a different level of check as follows.

1. *Basic disclosure* — this will reveal unspent convictions held at national level.
2. *Standard disclosure* — this level of check is for those in jobs which are exempted from the Rehabilitation of Offenders Act (see above). It reveals all convictions (whether spent or not), nationally held cautions, reprimands and warnings, as well as information contained on the Department of Health and the Department for Education lists of people considered unsuitable to work with children.
3. *Enhanced disclosure* — this level of check is available for jobs involving very close contact with children and vulnerable adults. As well as the information contained in a standard disclosure, it provides details from local police records if this is thought to be relevant to the position applied for.

In all cases, it is the job applicant who must apply to the DBS for disclosure. Basic disclosures are sent to the individual, who can then decide whether to show them to the employer. With standard and enhanced disclosures, both the job applicant and the prospective employer must sign the application, and copies of the disclosure are sent to both. Employers who wish to make use of this service must be registered with the DBS and signed up to their Code of Practice. The cost of registering is £300. The cost of a standard disclosure is £26. The cost of an enhanced disclosure is £44. Disclosures for volunteers in sensitive positions (ie work with children or vulnerable adults) are issued free of charge.

In Scotland, Disclosure Scotland fulfils similar functions to the DBS in England and Wales. Basic disclosures are available in Scotland to individual applicants at a cost of £25 and this same fee applies also to standard and enhanced checks in Scotland. Employers in Northern Ireland go through Access NI.

Vetting and Barring Scheme

Increased protection came into effect from 12 October 2009 so that, within five years, around five million more jobs and voluntary positions — including most NHS jobs — have become subject to checks. This should mean, the Government has said, that many more people posing a risk to children and vulnerable adults will be excluded from the workplace.

From October 2009 the **Safeguarding Vulnerable Groups Act 2006** created a centralised vetting system for people barred from working with children and/or vulnerable adults, in both paid and unpaid work. The scheme covers employees and volunteers in the education, care and health sectors. There are now two barring lists (for children and vulnerable adults respectively) which are administered by the DBS, rather than the three lists (Protection of Children Act (POCA), Protection of Vulnerable Adults (PoVA) and List 99 (for teachers)) previously maintained by two different Government departments. People included on the new lists are barred from a much wider range of jobs than before, particularly in areas of work with vulnerable adults such as in the NHS.

Employers that knowingly engage barred individuals in a job that constitutes a "regulated activity" are committing a criminal offence and are liable to fines of up to £5000 and/or up to six months' imprisonment. It is also a criminal offence for barred individuals to seek or undertake work with children or vulnerable adults.

Finally, a new duty to share information was introduced with employers, social services and professional regulators required to notify the DBS of relevant information so that individuals posing a threat to children or vulnerable adults can be barred.

Under the **Protection of Freedoms Act 2012**, the CRB and the ISA were merged to form a streamlined new body called the Disclosure and Barring Service providing a proportionate barring and criminal records checking service.

The Government has introduced portability of criminal record checks between jobs. A certificate issued after this date will be portable within the same type of workforce (eg a job that involves working with children). Registered employers are required to specify the type of workforce when completing an application for a DBS certificate.

Health and Safety

It is the duty of every employer to ensure the health and safety of every worker as far as is "reasonably practicable".

Administration

The main points are as follows.

- The rules are given in the **Health and Safety at Work, etc Act 1974** and subordinate legislation backed up by Codes of Practice approved by the Health and Safety Executive (HSE) and by Guidance Notes.
- The Act is concerned with real not hypothetical risks.
- The Act requires the employer to take safety steps and to provide information to employees.
- The HSE and local authorities appoint inspectors to ensure compliance.
- An inspector who finds a breach of the legislation may require the employer to comply. This may be done informally or by an improvement notice or a prohibition notice:
  - an improvement notice requires any remedy to be made within 21 days (this period may be extended)
  - a prohibition notice requires an activity to cease within a time limit which, in an emergency, can be immediately.
- The employer may appeal to a tribunal about either notice.
- Non-compliance with a notice can lead to prosecution in the magistrates' court.

General Provisions

All employers have a duty to:
- provide and maintain plant and systems of work which are safe and without undue risk
- ensure that the handling, storage and transport of materials is done safely
- see that the place of work is maintained in a safe condition
- see that there are safe entrances to and exits from the place of work
- ensure that the working environment is safe
- provide such information, instruction, training and supervision as is necessary to ensure the health and safety of employees.

The **Workplace (Health, Safety and Welfare) Regulations 1992** implement specific provisions concerning minimum health and safety requirements for the workplace. These and other regulations require that premises must:

- be registered and display a summary of relevant health and safety law and information on the enforcing authorities (for example, by displaying the HSE poster which has been approved for this purpose)
- be kept clean
- provide each worker with 11m^3 of space

- be heated to at least 16°C (13°C where severe physical effort is involved)
- be provided with a thermometer
- have adequate ventilation and lighting
- have adequate washing and toilet facilities (as defined)
- provide drinking water for employees
- have space for employees' outdoor clothing to be hung
- have a seat for every employee
- have a first-aid box and train first-aiders as specified
- have soundly constructed and properly maintained floors, stairs, steps, passageways and gangways
- have staircases with suitable and sufficient handrails, including a handrail on any open side
- have secure fencing around any dangerous machines or openings in the floor
- have suitable and easily accessible rest facilities
- have adequate fire precautions.

Visual Display Units (VDUs)

Under the **Health and Safety (Display Screen Equipment) Regulations 1992** (as amended) employers must:

- pay for an eye test for any employee who works with a VDU
- pay for any special corrective glasses needed to work with a VDU (ie where the employee's normal corrective glasses cannot be used).

They also have a duty to analyse VDU workstations (including equipment, furniture and the environment) for the purpose of assessing and reducing any health and safety risks. Equipment must be adjustable (eg chairs, screens and keyboards) and lighting must be such that the VDU screen is glare-free. In some cases, footrests and wrist rests may need to be provided.

It is also advisable to:

- warn staff about the risk of repetitive strain injury (RSI)
- allow a 5 or 10-minute break from screen work every hour where work cannot be organised to allow breaks or changes of activity.

Special Provisions

There are special provisions regarding reporting of injuries, first aid, noise, dangerous chemicals, radioactive materials, electricity, work equipment, machinery, personal protective equipment, lifting and dangerous activities such as diving. Details are included in *Reference Book for Employers*.

Working Time

The **Working Time Regulations 1998** (as amended) impose a number of restrictions on the working hours and periods of employment of most people who work (although certain groups are excluded from some or all of the provisions). As the law now stands:

- adult workers (ie workers aged 18 and over) have the right not to be required to work for more than an average of 48 hours a week (calculated over a reference period of 17 weeks, which may be increased to 26 weeks by their employer (but only in prescribed circumstances), or to up to 52 weeks under a collective or workforce agreement (but see the *Note* below)

- adolescent workers (ie workers under the age of 18), may not lawfully be employed for more than eight hours a day, or for more than 40 hours in any week (including overtime hours), with no provision for averaging

- adult workers may not lawfully be employed at night for more than an average of eight hours in any 24-hour period, calculated over a reference period of 17 weeks (see above), or, if engaged in hazardous activities, for more than eight hours in any 24-hour period (with no provision for averaging)

- adolescent workers may not lawfully be employed at night (other than in prescribed circumstances) between the hours of 2200 and 0600 (or between 2300 and 0700, if their contracts require them to work after 2200), with no provision for averaging

- night workers are entitled to free initial and follow-up health assessments (or, if under the age of 18, free initial and follow-up health and capacities assessments)

- every worker is entitled to a minimum weekly rest period of 24 hours (or 48 hours in every fortnight); or, if under the age of 18, a minimum weekly rest period of 48 consecutive hours

- every worker is entitled to a daily work-free rest period of a minimum of 11 consecutive hours; or, if under the age of 18, a minimum daily rest period of 12 consecutive hours

- every worker is entitled to a minimum 20-minute rest break during the course of any working day or shift lasting or expected to last for more than six hours; or, if under the age of 18, a minimum 30-minute rest break during the course of any working day or shift lasting, or expected to last, for more than four and a half hours

- every worker is entitled to a minimum of 5.6 weeks of paid leave in every holiday year (and to accrued holiday pay on the termination of his or her employment, even if employed for no more than one or two days).

Note: Adult workers may opt out of the average 48-hour week if, but only if, they do so voluntarily, individually and in writing (with no hint of pressure from their employers). The agreement must inform them of their right to cancel the agreement on giving their employer an agreed period of notice (not exceeding three months) but, in the absence of such a statement, the employee is entitled to cancel the agreement by giving the employer seven days' notice. The opt out option is not available to workers under the age of 18. Adults who work with a large degree of independence and determine their own hours are excluded from all the working time provisions except for the entitlement to paid annual leave.

Following various key decisions of the Court of Justice of the European Union (CJEU), the following principles have been established in respect of the relationship between sickness absence and statutory annual holiday entitlement.

- Statutory annual holiday continues to accrue during all periods of sickness absence (whatever their length).
- An employee who is absent from work due to incapacity must either be allowed, if he or she wishes, to take and be paid for accrued holidays while off sick or, alternatively, to take the accrued holiday entitlement after returning to work.
- If, due to sickness absence, the employee has not taken his or her full statutory annual holiday entitlement, the employer must allow the employee to carry forward up to four weeks of the untaken leave and take it during the next holiday year (or within a period of 18 months from the end of the leave year in which the holiday accrued).
- If the employment is terminated, the employer must make a payment to the employee in lieu of the accrued annual leave, even where the employee was off sick for the full holiday year.

The EAT has ruled (in *Plumb v Duncan Print Group Ltd* EAT 0071/15) that the law does not require employers to allow carry-over of statutory annual leave without limit. Any holiday leave that has been carried over as a result of sickness absence must be taken within a period of (at most) 18 months from the end of the holiday year in which the leave accrued, otherwise it is lost.

The 1998 Regulations are policed and enforced both by the employment tribunals (in relation to a worker's statutory rights to rest breaks, paid annual holidays, etc) and by the HSE (in relation to the limits on weekly working time, night work, etc). Any term in a contract of employment or related agreement that purports to override or undermine a worker's rights under those regulations is void and unenforceable.

Holiday Pay

The CJEU has ruled (in *Williams and ors v British Airways plc* [2011] IRLR 948) that employees on statutory annual leave must be paid a sum equivalent to their normal remuneration, and that holiday pay must therefore include any allowances which are "intrinsically linked" to performance of the workers' jobs, as well as any allowances related to their professional and personal status.

Subsequently, in *Lock v British Gas Trading* [2014] IRLR 648, the CJEU held that any commission that a worker would have earned (had he or she not been on holiday) must be incorporated into holiday pay. Then in *Bear Scotland Ltd v Fulton* [2014] EAT 0047/13, the EAT ruled in a case involving three conjoined claims that "non-guaranteed overtime" which is a regular and permanent feature of the employment must be factored into holiday pay. Non-guaranteed overtime is overtime that the employee is obliged to work if asked but which the employer is not obliged to offer. Furthermore, the EAT has ruled (in *Dudley Metropolitan Borough Council v Willetts and ors* EAT 0334/16) that overtime which was worked on a purely voluntary basis (and also standby and call-out payments) should be incorporated into workers' holiday pay as these pay elements were a regular and long-term feature of the workers' employment.

The combined effect of these cases is that the calculation of employees' holiday pay must include all elements of pay which are part of their normal remuneration, for example, allowances, sales commission and/ or regular overtime which the employee would normally have earned.

Note: These principles apply only to the first four weeks of statutory annual leave prescribed by EU law, and not to the 1.6 weeks' additional holiday to which employees are entitled under the **Working Time Regulations 1998**, nor to any further holiday entitlement that may be granted under employees' contracts.

Data Protection

Replacing the **Data Protection Act 1998** (DPA) the General Data Protection Regulation (GDPR) from 25 May 2018, introduces new, and in some cases more onerous, obligations for data controllers and processors. Backed by the threat of fines well in excess of those imposed for breaches of the DPA, it will require those responsible for personal data to adhere to the principle of protection "by design and by default". The GDPR will give individuals a series of rights including:

- to be informed
- of access to their personal data
- to rectification
- to erasure
- to restrict processing
- of data portability
- against the risk that a potentially damaging decision is taken without human intervention
- to object.

The overall aim is not only to ensure the same level of data protection across all the Member States but also to apply restrictions to organisations in non-EU countries who supply online services to and/or collect the personal data of citizens in the Union. This is one reason why it is generally agreed that the UK will continue to apply the GDPR even after Brexit. As the Institute of Directors (IoD) said: "This equivalence will be crucial to ensure digitally-minded UK firms can operate across the EU, their biggest trading partner".

Principles Relating to Processing of Personal Data

The DPA stipulated eight principles by which organisations must abide. However, the GDPR has condensed this requirement to six, as follows.
Personal data shall be:

- processed lawfully, fairly and in a transparent manner in relation to the data subject
- collected for specified, explicit and legitimate purposes and not further processed in a manner that is incompatible with those purposes; further processing for archiving purposes in the public interest, scientific or historical research purposes or statistical purposes shall not be considered to be incompatible with the initial purposes
- adequate, relevant and limited to what is necessary in relation to the purposes for which they are processed

- accurate and, where necessary, kept up to date, every reasonable step must be taken to ensure that personal data that are inaccurate, having regard to the purposes for which they are processed, are erased or rectified without delay
- kept in a form which permits identification of data subjects for no longer than is necessary for the purposes for which the personal data are processed; personal data may be stored for longer periods insofar as the personal data will be processed solely for archiving purposes in the public interest, scientific or historical research purposes or statistical purposes subject to implementation of the appropriate technical and organisational measures required by the GDPR in order to safeguard the rights and freedoms of the data subject
- processed in a manner that ensures appropriate security of the personal data, including protection against unauthorised or unlawful processing and against accidental loss, destruction or damage, using appropriate technical or organisational measures.

In short, therefore, the six principles are the following.

1. Lawfulness, fairness and transparency.
2. Purpose limitation.
3. Data minimisation.
4. Accuracy.
5. Storage limitation.
6. Integrity and confidentiality.

Data Protection and Employees

Employers will need to have regard to personal information collected from those who work for them. Under the GDPR, employees as data subjects will have greater rights and, although many of the new requirements are not dissimilar to those laid down under the DPA 1998, they are generally expanded. In this context, employees will have, under the GDPR, the right:

- to rectification of data that is inaccurate or incomplete
- to be forgotten under certain circumstances (where the data are no longer necessary for the purpose for which they were originally collected, for example)
- to be informed as to how their personal data will be used
- to data portability (that is, to obtain and reuse their personal data for their own purposes across different services)
- of access.

As several authorities have pointed out: "It is not enough to comply, you have to be seen to be complying". Employers would therefore be well advised to demonstrate clear compliance with regard to the use and protection of staff data including staff training in this area, allowing individuals to monitor processing, and keeping and giving access to all relevant documents on processing activities. They will need to be able to make clear why and how they collect, transfer and store employee data and may, therefore, wish to review internal HR policies with particular regard to vetting and assessment activities in recruitment.

Remember that the regulation states: "Personal data shall be collected for specified, explicit and legitimate purposes and not further processed in a manner that is incompatible with those purposes. Data must be adequate, relevant and limited to what is necessary in relation to the purposes for which they are processed (data minimisation)". In other words, employers must collect only such data for which need can be demonstrably proved — and no more. Furthermore, once the personal data is no longer required for the purpose for which it was collected, it should be deleted unless there are reasonable grounds for retaining it. This means there should be a review process in place including regular cleansing of HR databases.

Consent

If the data subject's consent is given in the context of a written declaration which also concerns other matters, then the GDPR insists that the request for consent must be presented: in a manner which is clearly distinguishable from those other matters; in an intelligible and easily accessible form; using clear and plain language. It must be as easy to withdraw consent as to give it. The ICO has offered guidance on this important point: "It follows that, if for any reason you cannot offer people a genuine choice over how you use their data, consent will not be an appropriate basis for processing. This may be the case if, for example, you are in a position of power over the individual — for example if you are a public authority or an employer processing employee data".

The guidance goes on to say that an organisation processing employee data would be advised to look for another basis for processing (rather than consent) such as "legitimate interests". Certainly, just adding a term about consenting to the use of personal data in a standard employment contract is unlikely to satisfy the terms of the GDPR.

Credit References

A separate law deals with keeping credit information on individuals. In practice this is held by a few large companies, which must register and which sell it to their customers. An individual has the right:

- to know from any party whether it has used a credit reference agency and, if so, which one
- to send that agency his or her name and address with £2, and receive a copy of all the data the agency has on that individual
- to have errors corrected, falsehoods removed and other relevant data added.

Computer Security

Under the **Computer Misuse Act 1990**, unauthorised use of computers, commonly known as "hacking", is illegal. The four offences are:
- deliberate, unauthorised access to computer programs or data
- unauthorised access with the intent to commit further offences
- intentionally modifying program or data during unauthorised access
- procuring someone else to hack into a computer.

Email, the Internet and Telephone Communications

Changes in the world of IT in recent years mean that the business use of email and the internet has grown considerably. Employers need a comprehensive policy on the use of telecommunications systems at work so that employees not only know what is permitted by way of personal use but are also made aware of the extent to which an employer may intercept communications.

The **Telecommunications (Lawful Business Practice) (Interception of Communications) Regulations 2000** came into force on 24 October 2000 and set out the circumstances in which employers can lawfully and without consent intercept, record and monitor emails and telephone calls. These regulations have been made under the **Regulation of Investigatory Powers Act 2000** (RIPA) which repealed the **Interception of Communications Act 1985**. RIPA also implemented Article 5 of the European Telecommunications Data Protection Directive which required the Member States to protect the confidentiality of communications and take account of the European Convention on Human Rights (ECHR).

The regulations allow employers to monitor or record telephone calls and emails, without consent, to:

- establish the existence of facts relevant to the business
- ensure compliance with regulatory practices and procedures
- prevent or detect crime
- monitor standards of service for quality control or staff training purposes
- detect unauthorised use of the system
- maintain the effective operation of the system.

They are also allowed to monitor, but not record, communications to check whether they are relevant to the business.

However, these interceptions are authorised only if the controller of the system has made all reasonable efforts to inform potential users that their communications may be intercepted.

Employers must also have regard to *Part 3* of the Information Commissioner's *Employment Practices Data Protection Code*. This covers the monitoring of workers' phone calls, emails, computer use and various other activities, and sets out recommendations on how the legal requirements of the Data Protection Act can be met. The code suggests that before deciding whether to monitor employees, employers should carry out an impact assessment. This involves:

- identifying the purpose of monitoring and the benefits it is likely to bring
- assessing the likely impact on workers and their relationship with the employer
- considering alternatives to monitoring
- taking into account the obligations that will arise, such as notifying workers about monitoring (unless covert monitoring can be justified — see below) and handling the information which is collected
- deciding whether monitoring can be justified.

If employers decide to go ahead with monitoring, they should have regard to the good practice recommendations which the code contains. As a general rule, monitoring must be open and transparent, and carried out with the knowledge of employees. The code says that covert monitoring should only be used in exceptional circumstances such as in connection with the prevention or detection of criminal activity or equivalent malpractice. The *Employment Practices Data Protection Code* is available at *https://ico.org.uk*.

Trade Unions

Recognition

A statutory recognition procedure applies when unions and employers are unable to reach agreement on recognition voluntarily. Recognition will normally be granted automatically where over half of the "bargaining unit" (ie the group of workers to be covered by recognition) are members of the union or, following a ballot, where a majority of the voters and at least 40% of those entitled to vote support recognition. This procedure does not apply to employers who have 20 or fewer workers. Recognition disputes are handled by the Central Arbitration Committee. Similar procedures apply when an employer seeks to derecognise a union. It is unlawful to victimise a worker by taking action short of dismissal against him or her and unfair to dismiss an employee or select him or her for redundancy on grounds related to the above procedure.

If a trade union is recognised (either voluntarily or through the statutory procedure), it acquires considerable rights as follows.

1. To negotiate with the employer about pay, working hours and holidays (this authority is given to a union when it acquires statutory recognition but may also be given voluntarily by the employer). If the employer agrees, negotiations may also extend to other issues such as recruitment, termination of employment, disciplinary matters or allocation of work.
2. To be consulted on occupational pensions, health and safety, redundancy and the transfer of ownership of a business.
3. To time off work for its officials and individual employee members.

Closed Shop

A closed shop (or union membership agreement) is an agreement between an employer and a trade union under which the employer agrees not to employ any person who is not (or refuses to be) a member of that trade union. Nowadays, such agreements are unlawful and cannot be used as an excuse for denying employment to (or for dismissing or penalising) any person who refuses to be, or remain, a member of a particular trade union or of any trade union (even if the union in question is a recognised independent trade union). Furthermore, an employer cannot lawfully demand any payment or make any deduction from a non-union employee's wages or salary as an alternative to the payment of trade union dues. The penalties in such cases can be severe.

Industrial Action

The law regarding official industrial action is now tightly regulated. The main points are as follows.

- The dispute must be a trade dispute (ie not against Government policy) and relate to the employer concerned (ie not in support of strikers of another employer).
- The action must be supported by a majority of members voting in a properly conducted secret postal ballot.
- The union must give the employer at least seven days' written notice of the date of the ballot and of any official industrial action that may result.
- The union must include sufficient information to enable the employer to make plans to deal with the consequences of any industrial action and provide information to those employees called upon to vote.
- The union should advise the employer of the categories, descriptions and workplace of the employees in question.
- The union must supply the employer with a sample voting paper.
- If the ballot is positive, the union must give the employer a further seven days' notice of strike action.
- If more than 50 members are balloted, the ballot must be independently scrutinised.
- The ballot is valid for up to four weeks (although this can be extended to eight weeks if both the union and employer agree that the dispute might be settled by further negotiation).

New rules regarding industrial action were brought into force in March 2017. The **Trade Union Act 2016** has considerably limited trade unions' freedom to initiate industrial action. The Act provides that in order for industrial action to be legal:

- 50% of union members who are entitled to vote in the industrial action ballot must vote (this is in addition to the existing requirement for a majority of those actually voting to vote in favour of industrial action)
- in certain important public services (including the health, education, transport, border security and fire sectors) 40% of members entitled to vote must vote in favour of industrial action (in addition to the majority of those actually voting)
- the minimum notice period for industrial action that a trade union must give to the employer was doubled from 7 to 14 days (unless both parties agree to seven days)
- there is a six-month limit on strike mandates

- voting papers have to include more detailed descriptions of the trade dispute and the proposed action
- changes to the rules on political funding contributions require new members to opt in rather than opt out of paying these contributions.

Consequences of Being on Strike

An employee on strike:
- is not entitled to pay or other benefits of employment
- loses the strike period from his or her record of continuous service; the strike does not break a period of continuous employment, but it is excluded in reckoning this service
- loses the right to receive tax refunds under PAYE

may not receive income support for him- or herself (if the striker claims it for his or her family, the Department for Work and Pensions (DWP) will assume that he or she is receiving strike pay from the trade union, whether he or she is or not).

It is unfair to dismiss an employee for taking part in lawfully organised industrial action during the so-called "protected" period. This period is the first 12 weeks of the strike, or longer if the employer has not taken reasonable steps to resolve the dispute. A striking employee may also bring a claim of unfair dismissal if he or she is dismissed while taking official industrial action and some, but not all, of the employees taking part in the action are dismissed or some, but not all, of them are offered reinstatement or re-engagement within three months of the employee's dismissal. Employees taking unofficial industrial action who are dismissed do not have the right (except in very limited circumstances) to claim unfair dismissal.

Blacklisting

Employers and employment agencies who use so-called "blacklists" of known trade union activists with a view to turning someone down for employment will be liable to pay the job applicant compensation of up to £83,682 (from April 2018) and be liable for prosecution with a fine of up to £5000.

Action Short of Dismissal

It is unlawful for employers to pressurise employees in connection with trade union membership and activities by subjecting them to any detriment. This includes anything detrimental or disadvantageous to the employee, eg forfeiture of a pay rise, denial of opportunities for overtime working, promotion, transfer or further training, etc arising out of any act or failure to act by the employer.

Information and Consultation

Under the **Information and Consultation of Employees Regulations 2004** employers are required to inform and consult their staff about a range of matters if they employ 50 or more staff.

Companies that already have information and consultation arrangements in place (eg staff committee or works council) can continue to use these provided they meet certain criteria and have already been approved by a majority of the workforce. However, they can still be open to challenge. If at least 40% of the workforce puts in a request for new procedures, the employer must enter into negotiations to set these up. If fewer than 40%, but at least 10%, of the workforce put in a request for new procedures, then the employer can either start negotiations or, instead, ballot the workforce on keeping the existing arrangements. In the ballot, if at least 40% of the workforce and the majority of those voting vote in favour of having new arrangements, the employer must start negotiations to set these up.

Companies which currently have no information or consultation arrangements in place must enter into negotiations to set up a forum if at least 10% of employees request this. The regulations leave it to employers and employees to agree on the structure, subject matter, method, frequency and timing of their new information and consultation procedures. The arrangement must, however, cover all employees and must set out the circumstances in which the employer will inform and consult the employees.

If, following a valid request from employees, the employer fails to agree an arrangement within six months, then a default procedure automatically applies. This means that an information and consultation committee has to be established with employee representatives elected by means of a ballot. Employers are then obliged to inform and consult their staff about:

- recent and probable developments in the company's activities and the financial state of the business
- the structure and probable development of employment within the organisation, especially where there is a threat to job security
- decisions likely to lead to substantial changes in work organisation or employees' contracts (eg terms and conditions).

Note: In the case of collective redundancies involving 20 or more employees or a TUPE business transfer, employers are already required to inform and consult with worker representatives.

In this situation, the employer can notify employee representatives that it is consulting under these arrangements rather than under the information and consultation rules. There is no need to consult under both procedures.

Works Councils

Regulations implementing the European Works Councils Directive (EWC) came into force in January 2000. Companies and groups with at least 1000 employees across the EEA and at least 150 employees in each of two or more Member States are affected. Specific procedures must be followed when employees in multinational companies ask for information and consultation arrangements to be established. Failure to reach agreement will result in the setting up of an EWC in accordance with a statutory model.

Regulations came into force in June 2011 governing how multinational organisations inform and consult their employees, including new obligations on central management, a right to receive necessary training and an increase (from £75,000–£100,000) in the maximum penalty for a failure to inform and consult.

Relevant Parts of Criminal Law

Relevant Crimes

The following crimes are most likely to arise in employment:

- *theft* — dishonest removal of another person's property with the intention of permanently depriving him or her of it
- *criminal damage* — destroying or damaging someone else's property deliberately or recklessly
- *forgery* — making a document which is not what it appears to be (including altering an existing document)
- *perjury* — making a false statement as a witness
- *violence* — killing, injuring or sexually abusing a person
- *unlawful imprisonment* — holding a person against his or her will
- *tax evasion* — withholding or falsifying information about tax

- *insider dealing* — using non-public information to buy or sell securities in a company
- *fraud* — gaining a pecuniary advantage by deception.

Disclosure Offences

There are three offences that must be reported to the authorities, regardless of any duty of confidentiality. A person who fails to report reasonable suspicion is him- or herself guilty of an offence. The offences are:

- treason
- terrorism
- drug trafficking.

When an Employee is Accused of an Offence

The following points should be noted if an employee is accused of a criminal offence.

1. The employer does not have to wait until the employee's trial before instigating disciplinary action (unless advised otherwise by the police).
2. It will be very important to comply with any in-house disciplinary procedure and also to adhere to the relevant provisions in the Acas Code of Practice on *Disciplinary and Grievance Procedures*.
3. The burden of proof for dismissal is simply reasonable grounds for believing — the "balance of probabilities". (A criminal offence must be proved beyond reasonable doubt, therefore a person can be fairly dismissed for a criminal offence even though he or she is acquitted in court.)
4. The offence does not have to be committed at work, but if committed outside of work, it must be relevant in some way to the person's employment, eg an offence which makes the individual unsuitable to perform his or her specific job duties or which is likely to bring the employer's name into disrepute.

The **Public Interest Disclosure Act 1998** protects "whistleblowers" from being dismissed or victimised by their employers for making a disclosure about criminal offences, breaches of legal obligation, miscarriages of justice, health and safety dangers, environmental risk or any cover-ups relating to such matters.

The protection only applies if the worker reasonably believes that the disclosure is in the public interest.

In April 2010 the Government amended the ET1 so that claimants to an employment tribunal can tick a box if they wish allegations of whistleblowing to be passed to the relevant authority.

Insolvency

Insolvency proceedings start when a person cannot pay his or her bills. An individual can become bankrupt, which means that most of his or her property is vested in a trustee who must pay the bankrupt's creditors what he or she can.

Broadly, a company can go into:
- *liquidation* — where the company is wound up and its assets sold
- *receivership* — where the company is kept going in the hope that bits of the business can be sold
- *administration* — where the company continues but its management is replaced.

Order of Debts

The creditors are paid in this order.
1. *Pre-preference debts* — fees and expenses of the liquidator or receiver.
2. *Preferential debts* — wages and taxes to a limit.
3. *Secured debts* — most formal loans.
4. *Unsecured debts* — most suppliers and all creditors not ranking higher.
5. *Proprietor or shareholders.*

Wages

An employee may claim in liquidation for:
- pay, bonuses and commissions due for the four-month period prior to the insolvency
- all accrued holiday pay
- statutory guarantee pay
- monies arising from a medical suspension
- time-off payments.

These are classed as a preferential debt to £800 per employee or (if less) four months' wages. Any balance outstanding ranks as an unsecured debt.

If an employee has any unpaid wages, he or she may claim from the State via the liquidator. The maximum claimable is eight weeks' pay up to the same figure as used for redundancy pay (currently £508 a week).

Special provisions also apply for the recovery of Statutory Sick Pay, Statutory Maternity/Paternity/Adoption and Shared Parental Pay, and Statutory Redundancy Payments.

Persons

Name

Broadly a person's name is what he or she wants it to be. The law is usually only concerned when a name is used to conceal a person's true identity.

A person may change his or her surname or family name at will for all purposes. A person cannot usually change his or her first or given name but may "be known" by any first or given name and surname or family name wished.

For employment purposes, the following is regarded as good practice when an employee advises the employer of a change of surname or family name. The employer should:

- accept a change when a woman adopts or abandons her husband's surname or family name on marriage or divorce (although this is only long-standing convention, not law)
- accept as conclusive any deed poll or statutory declaration sworn in front of a solicitor
- otherwise require a letter signed by a magistrate, doctor, vicar or person of similar standing who knows the person and confirms that the name has changed for all purposes.

Age

A person's age is the number of years which have elapsed from his or her birth to the beginning of his or her last birthday.

Sex

All humans are legally either male or female as they were born. However, it is unlawful under the **Equality Act 2010** to discriminate on grounds of gender reassignment. It is also unlawful under the Act to discriminate against workers or job applicants because of sexual orientation. This includes direct discrimination, indirect discrimination, victimisation and harassment. Employers are only allowed to treat employees differently because of their sexual orientation in very limited circumstances, such as where being of a particular sexual orientation is a genuine and determining occupational requirement for the job. Another is where employment is for the purposes of an organised religion and the requirement on sexual orientation is necessary in order to comply with the doctrines of the religion, or to avoid conflicting with followers' religious convictions. No minimum period of employment is needed to make a claim of sexual orientation discrimination. If a claim is upheld, the tribunal will make a declaration and award such compensation as it considers appropriate.

Marital Status

A person is either married, single or in a civil partnership. Bachelorhood, divorce, separation and widowhood are all versions of the single state.

A couple are married if:

- they have undergone a public legal ceremony and complied with the conditions of marriage
- (generally) have married overseas in accordance with that country's laws.

Note: Same-sex marriages became legal in England and Wales as from 29 March 2014 (under the **Marriage (Same Sex Couples) Act 2013**) and in **Scotland the Marriage and Civil Partnership (Scotland) Act 2014** allowed same-sex couples in Scotland to marry as from 31 December 2014.

A couple are civil partners if they are registered under the **Civil Partnership Act 2004**. A live-in partner is not a "common law" wife or husband. He or she has no marital rights.

The employment consequences of marriage are:

- personnel records need amending
- there may be a change of address and next of kin
- a woman may change her surname
- the person's tax code may change
- the employee may change the "statement of wish" regarding a pension lump sum
- the employer may make a tax-free wedding present to the employee.

The employment consequences of divorce are:

- personnel records need amending
- there may be a change of address and next of kin
- a woman may change her surname
- a man's tax code will change unless he is voluntarily maintaining his former wife

- a woman cannot continue paying reduced rate National Insurance contributions
- adjustments may be made to pension arrangements.

Religion

Employers must not discriminate against workers or job applicants because of religion or belief. The rules on this form of discrimination are set out in the **Equality Act 2010**. The regulations prohibit direct discrimination, indirect discrimination, victimisation and harassment. The regulations define "religion or belief" as being any religion, religious belief or philosophical belief. Employers can discriminate against job applicants or employees in very limited circumstances, such as where being of a particular religion or belief is a "genuine and determining occupational requirement" for the job in question. The employer must be able to show that it is proportionate to apply the religious requirement in that particular case.

There is also a special category of occupational requirement which applies to organisations with a particular religious ethos. In such cases, the requirement for a particular religion or belief does not have to be a "determining" factor for the job, so long as it is a requirement and it is proportionate to apply it in that particular case.

No minimum period of employment is needed to make a claim of religious discrimination. If the complaint is upheld, the tribunal will make a declaration and award such compensation as it considers appropriate.

Human Rights

The **Human Rights Act 1998** incorporates the rights and freedoms guaranteed under the European Court of Human Rights (ECHR) into UK law. People who believe that their human rights have been violated can have their cases judged in UK courts rather than in the ECHR in Strasbourg.

Some of the provisions of the European Convention on Human Rights are likely to have a particular impact on employment law. These include the right:

- to respect for private and family life, home and correspondence
- to freedom of thought, conscience and religion
- to freedom of expression
- to freedom of peaceful assembly and of association, including the right to form and join a trade union
- not to be discriminated against on certain grounds.

Public sector workers are directly affected whereas private sector workers have no direct rights under the Act. The provisions still affect them, however, because courts and tribunals have to interpret UK domestic law in a way which is compatible with the convention.

Death

The employment consequences of the death of an employee are:

- the employment ended with payment due to date of death
- it is courteous to express sympathy to the employee's family and to make a representation at the funeral
- any SMP is paid to the end of the week of death; SSP to the day of death
- outstanding payments must be made to the employee's personal representative including pay in lieu of any untaken statutory holidays
- HMRC is advised by sending all three parts of the P45 marked "D"
- no National Insurance is payable in the pay period of death
- the personal allowance for tax is claimed for the whole year, which can mean a substantial tax rebate, particularly if the death is early in the tax year
- the HSE must be informed without delay if an employee dies as a result of a work-related injury, or dies within 12 months of sustaining any such injury (as per the **Reporting of Injuries, Diseases and Dangerous Occurrences Regulations 1995**)
- a spouse's pension, life insurance claim or pension guarantee may become payable
- a survivor's pension may be payable to a surviving partner in a partnership registered under the **Civil Partnership Act 2005**
- the personnel records need amending
- if death occurred at work, notification to the HSE and the police must be made
- if the employee was under notice for what is held to be an unfair dismissal, the date of death is substituted for the date of dismissal
- any proceedings outstanding between employer and employee only continue if the personal representative so directs
- any tax rebates withheld for being on strike are paid.

Relations with Auditors, etc

Payroll and employment information should be regarded as confidential. It should only be divulged:

- to colleagues in the payroll or HR departments who need to know it

- to the employee him- or herself or someone the employee has authorised
- to the National Insurance contributions Office
- as ordered by a court
- to the company's auditor
- to BEIS inspectors conducting a formal investigation
- to HMRC
- as required by the DWP or Child Support Agency on submission of a written document
- when supplying a reference to another employer or prospective employer, though payroll information should normally not be given
- to the police if it is within their powers (employment and payroll data is generally "excluded material" which cannot be seized even when the police have a search warrant).

Note: Any person who gives false information to the above could be guilty of a criminal offence.

Insurance Requirements for Employers

An employer must:
- have at least £5 million in insurance cover for personal injury or disease sustained by employees during their employment
- conspicuously display the certificate on the premises
- keep insurance certificates for 40 years.

Courts and Tribunals

An employee has the right to bring proceedings against an employer before an employment tribunal. An appeal (including an appeal in a breach of contract case) may go from the employment tribunal to the Employment Appeal Tribunal (EAT).

With effect from 6 April 2014, prospective tribunal claimants must contact Acas with a view to early conciliation before submitting a claim to the employment tribunal. A claimant can only lodge a claim with the tribunal after Acas has provided an early conciliation certificate containing a unique reference number which has to be entered on to the tribunal claim form (form ET1). There is, however, no obligation on either party to engage in the conciliation process or to settle. Where the parties do engage in conciliation, it may continue for up to one month, and may sometimes be extended for up to two further weeks. The relevant time limits for lodging claims with the tribunal are put on hold during the period that the claim is with Acas.

Settlement Outside a Tribunal

Two legal processes exist for achieving binding settlements outside a tribunal.

The first is provided by Acas which has a duty to conciliate and try to settle claims after they have been brought to the employment tribunal. A settlement is recorded on a form COT3. Acas will only act if brought in early and will not formalise an already agreed settlement.

The second process is a settlement agreement (previously known as "compromise agreement"). This is valid if:

- it is made in writing
- the settlement relates to the particular dispute
- it is made after the employee has received independent legal advice
- it states that the conditions regulating settlement agreements are satisfied
- the relevant independent advisor is either a qualified lawyer, a certified trade union official or advice centre worker
- the advice is covered by a policy of insurance or professional indemnity.

For more details, see *Reference Book for Employers*.

Tribunal

A tribunal usually comprises three members:

- an independent, legally qualified employment judge
- a lay member drawn from a panel of employer members
- a lay member drawn from a panel of employee members.

In some cases an employment judge may hear the matter alone.

Conduct of the Tribunal

The procedure is broadly:

- one party (the claimant) submits an ET1 claim form (after having contacted Acas for early conciliation — see above)
- employment judges conduct an initial paper sift or "consideration" of all claim forms and response forms in order to establish whether the claim (or the defence, as the case may be) is weak
- a preliminary hearing may be set up for a variety of reasons, eg to determine whether the tribunal has jurisdiction to hear the case, hold case management discussions, and/or consider an application for a deposit or for the case or defence to be struck out
- if the claim has no reasonable prospect of success, a tribunal may require a deposit of up to £1000 before continuing
- the other party (the respondent) is sent a copy of the claim and invited to submit a defence ET3, a copy of which is then sent to the claimant

- either party may ask for more information from the other
- either side may ask the tribunal to make an order for further particulars
- either side must give the other a copy of any document to be used at a hearing
- at the hearing each side presents its case, including submitting documents and calling witnesses
- the tribunal may, at any stage of the proceedings, strike out either the claim or the defence (or part of it) on the grounds that it is vexatious, unreasonable or misconceived, or in circumstances where one of the parties has conducted the proceedings in a manner that is vexatious, abusive, disruptive or otherwise unreasonable
- the hearing is held in public unless the employment judge decides otherwise
- either side may represent themselves or be suitably represented
- the claimant usually starts proceedings by presenting his or her case
- the proceedings are informal and the scope of acceptable evidence wide
- each party may cross-examine the other's witnesses
- the employment judge has the power (at his or her discretion) to timetable the evidence, ie allocate a maximum amount of time that each party has to present their evidence and their final submissions
- at the end, each party summarises its case
- the tribunal issues a decision or may take time to consider a decision
- tribunals have the power to make a costs order against either party for any costs incurred by the other party in certain defined circumstances (although in most cases, the parties pay their own costs).

Appeals

A dissatisfied party may appeal to:
- the tribunal, if the party believes an important detail has been overlooked or new evidence comes to light
- the EAT on a point of law, or if the party believes that the decision is "perverse".

Reform of Tribunal System

The Government made various changes to the employment tribunal process from 6 April 2012. In summary, these were as follows.
- Employment judges can sit alone to hear unfair dismissal claims.
- Employment judges can order a party calling a witness to cover that witness' costs in certain circumstances.

- Witness statements may be taken as read unless there has been an order given to the contrary.
- The level of deposit that a tribunal can order either of the parties to pay in circumstances where the tribunal believes that the party in question has little prospect of success was increased from £500 to £1000.
- The level of costs that can be awarded against one of the parties was increased from £10,000 to £20,000.

If the costs award is £20,000 or less, the tribunal may make the award without conducting a detailed assessment. Awards for over £20,000 may either be assessed by the employment judge or alternatively he or she may refer the matter on to the relevant civil court for a detailed assessment.

CHAPTER 7

Statistics

Retail Prices Index

Popularly known as the "cost of living index" or "retail price index", this index is designed to show the monthly change in the average level of prices of commodities that are considered necessary for the day-to-day existence of practically all wage earners and most small and medium salary earners and is issued monthly by the Office for National Statistics.

The official index figure is calculated in respect of the Tuesday nearest to the 15th of the month. A period of about four to five weeks is required to collect and summarise the prices and to calculate the "all items" figure, which is released some time between the 16th and the 26th of the month for the previous month.

The table below shows monthly movements in the index.

General Index of Retail Prices (RPI) (Prices at January 1987 = 100)

Year	Month	Index	Inflation rate ++
2017	January	265.5	2.6
	February	268.4	3.2
	March	269.3	3.1
	April	270.6	3.5
	May	271.7	3.7
	June	272.3	3.7
	July	272.9	3.6

Year	Month	Index	Inflation rate ++
	August	274.7	3.9
	September	275.1	3.9
	October	275.3	4.0
	November	275.8	3.9
	December	278.1	4.1
2018	January	276.0	4.0
	February	278.1	3.6
	March	278.3	3.3

++ Percentage change over previous year.

The "cost of living index" first started in 1914 but it was not until 1947 that the index started on a proper up-to-date weighting basis. It was introduced at 100 in June 1947 and reached 153.4 by January 1956. In January 1956 the index started on a new basis of 100 based on the Household Expenditure enquiry held in 1953 and this index continued until 1962. In January of that year, and again in January 1974, the index base was reset at 100. The current index has January 1987 as its base. This base applies to index figures from February 1987 onwards. Details on the method of construction of the index are available from the Office for National Statistics.

Consumer Prices Index

The consumer prices index (CPI) is the main UK domestic measure of consumer price inflation for macroeconomic purposes. It forms the basis for the Government's target for inflation that the Bank of England's Monetary Policy Committee (MPC) is required to achieve.

From April 2011 the CPI will also be used for the indexation of benefits, tax credits and public service pensions.

Internationally, the CPI is known as the Harmonised Index of Consumer Prices (HICP). HICPs are calculated in each Member State of the European Union, according to rules specified in a series of European regulations developed by Eurostat in conjunction with the EU Member States. HICP's are used to compare inflation rates across the European Union. Since January 1999 it has also been used by the European Central Bank (ECB) as the measure of price stability across the euro area.

The CPI and the RPI are compiled using the same underlying price data, based on a large and representative selection of around 650 individual goods and services for which price movements are measured in around 150 randomly selected areas throughout the UK. Around 180,000 separate price quotations are used every month to compile the indices. The outlets in which the prices are collected are selected randomly. Expenditure weights are held constant for one year at a time.

The selection of goods and services that are priced to compile the CPI and RPI is reviewed annually. The contents of the 2017 basket are described in an article published on the Office for National Statistics website (*www.ons.gov.uk*).

Year	Month	Index	% change over previous year
2017	January	101.4	1.8
	February	102.1	2.3
	March	102.5	2.3
	April	102.9	2.7
	May	103.3	2.9
	June	103.3	2.6
	July	103.2	2.6
	August	103.8	2.9
	September	104.1	3.0
	October	104.2	3.0
	November	104.6	3.1
	December	104.9	3.0
2018	January	104.4	3.0
	February	104.9	2.7
	March	105.0	2.5

From the release of January consumer price inflation data on 16 February 2016, CPI and CPIH indices were re-referenced and published with 2015 = 100.

Historical Tables

Tables 1 and 2 below provide the Retail Prices Index (RPI) figures and the Tax and Price Index (TPI) figures respectively between January 1995 and December 2000.

Table 1: General Index of Retail Prices (Prices at January 1987 = 100)

Year	Jan	Feb	Mar	Apr	May	June	July	Aug	Sept	Oct	Nov	Dec
1995	146.0	146.9	147.5	149.0	149.6	149.8	149.1	149.9	150.6	149.8	149.8	150.7
1996	150.2	150.9	151.5	152.6	152.9	153.0	152.4	153.1	153.8	153.8	153.9	154.4
1997	154.4	155.0	155.4	156.3	156.9	157.5	157.5	158.5	159.3	159.5	159.6	160.0
1998	159.5	160.3	160.8	162.6	163.5	163.4	163.0	163.7	164.4	164.5	164.4	164.4
1999	163.4	163.7	164.1	165.2	165.6	165.6	165.1	165.5	166.2	166.5	166.7	167.3
2000	166.6	167.5	168.4	170.1	170.7	171.1	170.5	170.5	171.7	171.6	172.1	172.2

Table 2: Tax and Price Index (TPI) (January 1987 = 100)

Year	Jan	Feb	Mar	Apr	May	June	July	Aug	Sept	Oct	Nov	Dec
1995	137.2	138.2	138.8	140.3	141.0	141.2	140.4	141.3	142.0	141.2	141.2	142.1
1996	141.6	142.3	143.0	141.7	142.0	142.1	141.5	142.2	143.0	143.0	143.1	143.6
1997	143.6	144.2	144.6	143.8	144.4	145.0	145.0	146.0	146.9	147.1	147.2	147.6
1998	147.1	147.9	148.4	149.7	150.6	150.5	150.1	150.8	151.5	151.6	151.5	151.5
1999	150.5	150.8	151.2	151.2	151.7	151.7	151.1	151.5	152.7	152.6	152.8	153.4
2000	152.7	153.7	154.6	155.7	156.3	156.7	156.1	156.1	157.3	157.2	157.7	157.8

Average Weekly Earnings

The Average Weekly Earnings (AWE) measure replaced the Index of Average Earnings from November 2009, following its accreditation as a national statistic by the UK Statistics Authority. It is felt that the AWE offers a better measure of changes in the average wage of the economy.

The AWE table is compiled by the Office for National Statistics (ONS) from a monthly sample survey of gross wages and salaries paid in both the public and private sectors. Earnings covered by the survey include

STATISTICS

overtime, bonuses, commission, etc for all types of employee (manual, non-manual, full time, part time, etc).

The Index of Average Earnings is no longer published as it has ceased to be the headline measure of earnings growth.

The latest seasonally adjusted Index, including the headline estimates of earnings growth based on the Monthly Wages and Salaries Survey, can be downloaded from *http://bit.ly/2GadA13*.

Bank Base Rates

Current Official Bank Rate 0.5%

Date Changed	Rate
Thursday, 02 November 2017	0.5000
Thursday, 04 August 2016	0.2500
Thursday, 05 March 2009	0.5000
Thursday, 05 February 2009	1.0000
Thursday, 08 January 2009	1.5000
Thursday, 04 December 2008	2.0000
Thursday, 06 November 2008	3.0000
Wednesday, 08 October 2008	4.5000
Thursday, 10 April 2008	5.0000
Thursday, 07 February 2008	5.2500
Thursday, 06 December 2007	5.5000
Thursday, 05 July 2007	5.7500
Thursday, 10 May 2007	5.5000
Thursday, 11 January 2007	5.2500
Thursday, 09 November 2006	5.0000
Thursday, 03 August 2006	4.7500
Thursday, 04 August 2005	4.5000
Thursday, 05 August 2004	4.7500
Thursday, 10 June 2004	4.5000
Thursday, 06 May 2004	4.2500
Thursday, 05 February 2004	4.0000

Date Changed	Rate
Thursday, 06 November 2003	3.7500
Thursday, 10 July 2003	3.5000
Thursday, 06 February 2003	3.7500
Thursday, 08 November 2001	4.0000
Thursday, 04 October 2001	4.5000
Tuesday, 18 September 2001	4.7500
Thursday, 02 August 2001	5.0000
Thursday, 10 May 2001	5.2500
Thursday, 05 April 2001	5.5000
Thursday, 08 February 2001	5.7500
Thursday, 10 February 2000	6.0000
Thursday, 13 January 2000	5.7500
Thursday, 04 November 1999	5.5000
Wednesday, 08 September 1999	5.2500
Thursday, 10 June 1999	5.0000
Thursday, 08 April 1999	5.2500
Thursday, 04 February 1999	5.5000
Thursday, 07 January 1999	6.0000
Thursday, 10 December 1998	6.2500
Thursday, 05 November 1998	6.7500
Thursday, 08 October 1998	7.2500
Thursday, 04 June 1998	7.5000
Thursday, 06 November 1997	7.2500
Thursday, 07 August 1997	7.0000
Thursday, 10 July 1997	6.7500
Friday, 06 June 1997	6.5000
Tuesday, 06 May 1997	6.2500
Wednesday, 30 October 1996	5.9375
Thursday, 06 June 1996	5.6875

Date Changed	Rate
Friday, 08 March 1996	5.9375
Thursday, 18 January 1996	6.1250
Wednesday, 13 December 1995	6.3750
Thursday, 02 February 1995	6.6250
Wednesday, 07 December 1994	6.1250
Monday, 12 September 1994	5.6250
Tuesday, 08 February 1994	5.1250
Tuesday, 23 November 1993	5.3750
Tuesday, 26 January 1993	5.8750
Friday, 13 November 1992	6.8750
Friday, 16 October 1992	7.8750
Tuesday, 22 September 1992	8.8750

Inflation Rates

Inflation

	Jan	Feb	Mar	Apr	May	Jun	Jul	Aug	Sep	Oct	Nov	Dec
2018	3.0	2.7	2.5									
2017	1.8	1.8	2.3	2.3	2.7	2.9	2.6	2.6	2.9	3.0	3.1	3.0
2016	0.3	0.3	0.5	0.3	0.3	0.5	0.6	0.6	1.0	0.9	1.2	1.6
2015	0.3	0.0	0.0	-0.1	0.1	0.0	0.1	0.0	-0.1	-0.1	0.1	0.2
2014	1.9	1.7	1.6	1.8	1.5	1.9	1.6	1.5	1.2	1.3	1.0	0.5
2013	2.7	2.8	2.8	2.4	2.7	2.9	2.8	2.7	2.7	2.2	2.1	2.0
2012	3.6	3.4	3.5	3.0	2.8	2.4	2.6	2.5	2.2	2.7	2.7	2.7
2011	5.1	5.5	4.0	4.5	4.5	4.2	4.4	4.5	5.2	5.0	4.8	4.2
2010	3.7	3.7	4.4	5.3	5.1	5.0	4.8	4.7	4.6	4.5	4.7	4.8
2009	0.1	0.0	-0.4	-1.2	-1.1	-1.6	-1.4	-1.3	-1.4	-0.8	0.3	2.4
2008	4.1	4.1	3.8	4.2	4.3	4.6	5.0	4.8	5.0	4.2	3.0	0.9
2007	4.2	4.6	4.8	4.5	4.3	4.4	3.8	4.1	3.9	4.2	4.3	4.0
2006	2.4	2.4	2.4	2.6	3.0	3.3	3.3	3.4	3.6	3.7	3.9	4.4
2005	3.2	3.2	3.2	3.2	2.9	2.9	2.9	2.8	2.7	2.5	2.4	2.2

	Jan	Feb	Mar	Apr	May	Jun	Jul	Aug	Sep	Oct	Nov	Dec
2004	2.6	2.5	2.6	2.5	2.8	3.0	3.0	3.2	3.1	3.3	3.4	3.5
2003	2.9	3.2	3.1	3.1	3.0	2.9	3.1	2.9	2.8	2.6	2.5	2.8
2002	1.3	1.0	1.3	1.5	1.1	1.0	1.5	1.4	1.7	2.1	2.6	2.9
2001	2.7	2.7	2.3	1.8	2.1	1.9	1.6	2.1	1.7	1.6	0.9	0.7
2000	2.0	2.3	2.6	3.0	3.1	3.3	3.3	3.0	3.3	3.1	3.2	2.9
1999	2.4	2.1	2.1	1.6	1.3	1.3	1.3	1.1	1.1	1.2	1.4	1.8
1998	3.3	3.4	3.5	4.0	4.2	3.7	3.5	3.3	3.2	3.1	3.0	2.8
1997	2.8	2.7	2.6	2.4	2.6	2.9	3.3	3.5	3.6	3.7	3.7	3.6
1996	2.9	2.7	2.7	2.4	2.2	2.1	2.2	2.1	2.1	2.7	2.7	2.5
1995	3.3	3.4	3.5	3.3	3.4	3.5	3.5	3.6	3.9	3.2	3.1	3.2
1994	2.5	2.4	2.3	2.6	2.6	2.6	2.3	2.4	2.2	2.4	2.6	2.9
1993	1.7	1.8	1.9	1.3	1.3	1.2	1.4	1.7	1.8	1.4	1.4	1.9
1992	4.1	4.1	4.0	4.3	4.3	3.9	3.7	3.6	3.6	3.6	3.0	2.6
1991	9.0	8.9	8.2	6.4	5.8	5.8	5.5	4.7	4.1	3.7	4.3	4.5
1990	7.7	7.8	8.1	9.4	9.7	9.8	9.8	10.6	10.9	10.9	9.4	9.3

CHAPTER 8

Calendars

Bank and Public Holidays

Dates with asterisks are bank holidays which have been introduced since the 1971 Banking and Financial Dealings Act and are routinely proclaimed by the Queen. All other dates have been designated as bank holidays under the **Banking and Financial Dealings Act 1971**.

Bank and Public Holidays in England and Wales: 2018–2019

Holidays	2018	2019
New Year's Day (or day in lieu of New Year's Day)*	1 January	1 January
Good Friday	30 March	19 April
Easter Monday	2 April	22 April
Early May Bank Holiday	7 May	6 May
Spring Bank Holiday*	28 May	27 May
Summer Bank Holiday	27 August	26 August
Christmas Day (or in lieu of 25 December)	25 December	25 December
Boxing Day (or in lieu of 26 December)	26 December	26 December

*Designated bank holidays under the **Banking and Financial Dealings Act 1971**.

Bank and Public Holidays in Scotland: 2018–2019

Holidays	2018	2019
New Year's Day (or day in lieu of New Year's Day)	1 January	1 January
2 January (or day in lieu of 2 January)	2 January	2 January
Good Friday	30 March	19 April
Early May Bank Holiday	7 May	6 May
Spring Bank Holiday*	28 May	27 May
Summer Bank Holiday	6 August	5 August
St Andrew's Day (or in lieu of)	30 November	2 December
Christmas Day (or in lieu of 25 December)	25 December	25 December
Boxing Day (or in lieu of 26 December)	26 December	26 December

*Subject to Royal Proclamation.

Bank and Public Holidays in Northern Ireland: 2018–2019

Holidays	2018	2019
New Year's Day (or day in lieu of New Year's Day)	1 January	1 January
St Patrick's Day (or in lieu of 17 March)	19 March	18 March
Good Friday	30 March	19 April
Easter Monday (or in lieu of)	2 April	22 April
Early May Bank Holiday	7 May	6 May
Spring Bank Holiday	28 May	27 May
Battle of the Boyne (Orangemen's Day)	*12 July*	*12 July*
Summer Bank Holiday	27 August	26 August

Holidays	2018	2019
Christmas Day (or in lieu of 25 December)	25 December	25 December
Boxing Day (or in lieu of 26 December)	26 December	26 December

Dates in italics are subject to Proclamation by the Secretary of State for Northern Ireland and are not included in the Royal Proclamation.

Bank and Public Holidays in the Republic of Ireland: 2018–2019

Holidays	2018	2019
New Year's Day (or day in lieu of New Year's Day)	1 January	1 January
St Patrick's Day (or in lieu of 17 March)	19 March	18 March
Easter Monday (or in lieu of)	2 April	22 April
Public Holiday	7 May	6 May
Public Holiday	4 June	3 June
Public Holiday	6 August	5 August
Public Holiday	29 October	28 October
Christmas Day (or in lieu of 25 December)	25 December	25 December
St Stephen's Day (or in lieu of 26 December)	26 December	26 December

Religious Holidays and Festivals

Some dates are approximate and may vary by a day either side of the one stated. In most cases they are subject to the visibility of the new moon at Mecca and the traditions of the local community.

These are the main dates in the Hindu calendar.

Hindu Religious Holidays and Festivals: 2018–2019

Holidays	2018	2019
Makar Sankranti	14 January	15 January
Holi	2 March	21 March
Diwali	7 November	27 October

Islamic Religious Holidays and Festivals: 2018–2019

Holidays	2018	2019
Ramadan, First day of	16 May	5 May
Eid-ul-Fitr	15 June	4 June
Eid-ul-Adha	22 August	11 August
New Year Al Hijra	11 September	1 September
Ashura	20 September	9 September

Sikh Religious Holidays and Festivals: 2018–2019

Holidays	2018	2019
Birthday of Guru Gobind Singh	5 January	5 January
Hola Mohalla	2 March	22 March
Vaisakhi	14 April	14 April
Divali	7 November	22 October

The dates for Sikh festivals are taken from the Nanakshahi calendar.

Jewish Religious Holidays and Festivals: 2018–2019

Holidays	2018	2019
Passover (Pesach) (1st day)	31 March	19 April
New Year (Rosh Hashanah)	9 September	29 September

Holidays	2018	2019
Day of Atonement (Yom Kippur)	18 September	8 October
Festival of Lights (Hanukkah)	3 December	22 December

All Jewish holidays begin at sundown the day before that shown.

Chinese Religious Holidays and Festivals: 2018–2019

Holidays	2018	2019
Lunar New Year	16 February	5 February

Because the start of the Chinese New Year is based on lunar cycles, it can occur anywhere between late January and the middle of February.

CHAPTER 9

Payroll Procedures

Calculation of Gross Pay

Gross pay is usually calculated in one of three ways:
- by reference to an hourly, weekly or monthly rate
- according to units of production ("piece rate")
- by reference to hours worked.

Any one of these may be subject to additions for bonuses or commissions. The payroll department must know, for each employee:
- the basis of determining gross pay
- the relevant rate payable
- (for the hours worked or units of production methods), the hours worked or pieces produced
- any absences for the period (eg unpaid leave).

All such notifications must be appropriately authorised in writing and retained.

Inclusions for Income Tax

Income tax is charged under PAYE on:
- gross pay
- plus other payments from employer to employee, unless this is a reimbursement of expenses covered by the statutory exemption for paid or reimbursed expenses or, before April 2016, covered by an HM Revenue & Customs (HMRC) dispensation
- plus cash vouchers and pay in the form of readily convertible assets
- less contributions to a registered pension fund under a net pay arrangement

- less the cost of partnership shares purchased under a share incentive plan
- less amounts given under a payroll giving (Give As You Earn) scheme. Taxable non-cash benefits, such as a company car, are not taxed as gross income, but are taxed by an adjustment in the person's tax code. From 2016/17, there is statutory framework for voluntary payrolling, so employers can elect to report the value of most benefits in kind, such as a company car, through real-time information so that tax on the benefit can be collected through the payroll.

Inclusions for National Insurance

National Insurance (NI) is charged on:
- gross pay
- plus other payments from employer to employee, unless it is a reimbursement of expenses covered by the statutory exemption for paid or reimbursed expenses or, before April 2016, covered by an HMRC dispensation
- plus cash vouchers, pay in the form of readily convertible assets and most non-cash vouchers
- plus the amount of tax paid by the employer on the grossed up amount of an award that attracts Class 1 National Insurance under the Taxed Award Scheme
- less the cost of partnership shares purchased under a share incentive plan.

For NI purposes, the payroll department does not deduct:
- contributions to a registered pension fund
- amounts given under a payroll giving scheme.

Deductions from Pay

Deductions from pay may only be made if permissible within the law.
  The order of deductions is as follows.
Basic gross pay:
- deduct overpayments of previous gross pay (if allowed).
Gross pay:
- deduct income tax
- deduct NI.
Net pay:
- deduct attachment of earnings orders

- deduct student loan deductions under plan type 1 or plan type 2
- deduct amounts authorised by the employee in advance of wages being paid.

Take-home pay.

Vouchers

The taxation and NI treatment of vouchers is summarised below.

Tax and National Insurance Treatment of Vouchers

Use of voucher	Income tax	National Insurance
Exchangeable for cash	Taxable under PAYE	NIC able
Childcare voucher	First £55 pw (£50 for 2005/06): tax free except for employees who are higher or additional rate taxpayers who first received childcare vouchers on or after 6 April 2011. The limits then are £28 and £25 respectively. Vouchers for tax-exempt benefits are generally tax free and NI free	NI free
	Excess: taxable as a benefit	NIC able
Other voucher for goods or services	Taxable as a benefit	NIC able

The employer is responsible for making an estimate of earnings to determine the level of exemption for childcare vouchers at the start of the tax year or when the employee joins an employer run childcare voucher scheme. From 6 April 2018, childcare voucher schemes are closed to new entrants.

Determining Holiday Entitlement

Since 1 October 1998 all workers are entitled under the **Working Time Regulations 1998** to four weeks' paid annual holiday. As well as this statutory entitlement, many employees are entitled to holidays and holiday pay under the terms of their contracts of employment.

Entitlement to public holidays is currently determined by the contract of employment and as with other contractual holiday, this can be set against the entitlement to statutory holiday.

The amount of statutory holiday comprises the equivalent of four weeks plus eight days' public holidays (28 days), ie 5.6 weeks.

It is necessary to determine:

- the holiday entitlement for each employee
- how that entitlement accrues (eg *pro rata* through the leave year)
- the policy for employees in starting and leaving years.

When adjusting a monthly or annual salary for holidays, a day's pay is determined by a relevant clause in the employment contract.

Adjustments on Starting and Leaving

Starting

An employee who starts work will usually receive a *pro rata* payment for the first period worked, if paid on a weekly or monthly basis.

Leaving

An employee who leaves will usually receive a *pro rata* payment for the final period worked if paid on a weekly or monthly basis.

Any termination payments must be subject to tax and NI in accordance with their nature.

An adjustment may be made for any excess holiday taken. Under the **Working Time Regulations 1998**, where employment comes to an end during the leave year, pay in lieu must be given for any proportion of statutory holiday which has not been taken. The sum due can either be specified in an agreement or calculated according to a formula specified in the regulations. The regulations also set out detailed notice rules.

Adjustments for Unauthorised Absence

An employee has no right to take absence other than that which is allowed by law or contract. Even unpaid leave must be authorised. There are special provisions for industrial action.

Unauthorised absence will usually be adjusted for by the deduction of one day's pay for each day's absence.

Overtime

Overtime is a payment for working hours additional to those the employee is contracted to work.

The main points to note are as follows.

- An employee is not entitled to any overtime payment just because he or she worked the overtime. His or her entitlement requires a contractual right or agreement from the employer before the overtime was worked.
- Overtime is usually paid on an hourly basis. This can mean the calculation of the hourly rate for employees usually paid on a weekly or monthly basis.
- Overtime is not usually paid to piece workers. They are simply paid the going rate for the additional pieces of work produced.
- Overtime can attract an additional payment — the "overtime premium" — for working unsocial hours. Again, the employee only has an entitlement to an overtime premium if such is given in a contract of employment or agreed by employer before the overtime is worked.

Back Pay

Back pay is the amount of a retrospective pay rise, eg in July a 3% pay rise is agreed, backdated to April.

To pay back pay it is necessary to determine which employees are covered. For each employee, the payroll department must:

- determine whether the employee was employed for the whole period covered by the back pay
- establish the rate or other basis for the retrospective award
- calculate the amount of back pay, usually by multiplying the amounts paid in previous months by the retrospective pay increase
- add the back pay to gross pay for the week or month in which the back pay is paid. Back pay is subject to tax and NI in the week or month of payment, regardless of the period covered by the retrospective pay award.

Payroll Errors

Generally if a mistake is made on a payslip, it can be corrected on the next payslip. However, there are some mistakes which cannot be rectified so simply.

If the mistake meant that the employee received less pay than he or she should have, the employer should be willing to make an advance to cover the shortfall.

If the mistake meant the employee received more than he or she was due, the employer's right to reclaim the money depended on whether the mistake was one of fact or law.

However, the House of Lords ruled (in *Kleinwort Benson Ltd v Lincoln City Council* [1998] UKHL 38) that money paid under a mistake of law can be recovered, even where the payment has been made under a settled understanding of the law which is afterwards changed by a decision of the courts. There is no longer a distinction between a mistake of fact or law.

If the mistake was one of fact or law, the employer may only reclaim the money if:

- the employer had not led the employee to believe the money was his or hers
- the employee had not spent the money when the mistake was discovered, ie changed his or her financial position
- the mistake was not primarily caused by a mistake of the employee.

Time and Attendance

Time and attendance is a system for automatically recording a person's attendance at work. This ranges from simple "clocking in" to more sophisticated, computer-based flexible working systems.

The employer introducing such a system must decide:

- for the purposes of the **Working Time Regulations 1998** what constitutes working time and what constitutes rest breaks in order to ensure that a worker's average working time, including overtime, does not exceed 48 hours normally averaged over 17 weeks
- whether the employee must clock off for lunch and coffee breaks
- a policy for dealing with lateness
- a policy for paying overtime
- arrangements for dealing with all forms of authorised absence
- arrangements for dealing with forms of unauthorised absence (other than non-payment of wages for the day)
- systems for recording work at a different location
- what rules are needed to prevent clocking in by colleagues.

Advances on Wages

An advance of wages may be made at the employer's discretion. The following points should be noted.

- There should be a good reason for making the advance, such as covering a change from weekly to monthly pay.
- If the advance is to help the employee with his or her own financial difficulties, the employer should consider whether the advance will help the situation. The employee may be better served by financial counselling.
- The amount of the advance must be agreed with the employee.
- The employee must provide a written acknowledgement or receipt for the advance and written authorisation for the amount to be deducted from the next payslip or payslips. If the authorisation is not signed, the employer has no right to deduct the amount.
- The advance is not subject to tax or NI or other deductions.
- The next payslip is calculated in the normal way. The amount of the advance is deducted from net pay after all other deductions.
- If advances are made frequently, they will be regarded as a regular payment and then be subject to tax and NI. What constitutes "frequently" is not defined, although more than twice in one year has been suggested.

Payment Methods

Payment may be made by:

- cash
- cheque
- credit transfer.

An employee cannot generally insist on being paid in cash. While persuasion is clearly the best policy, it is possible that some employees will still refuse to accept a change in pay method. Some individuals are stubborn about giving up any right, however worthless the right is in reality. In such circumstances, the employer may decide unilaterally to impose cashless pay.

While this would be a clear breach of contract, in reality there is little the employee can do about it. The only legal remedy would be to leave the employment immediately on the grounds that the employer's breach was so serious and fundamental to the employment relationship continuing that a claim of unfair constructive dismissal is made in the hope that an employment tribunal would regard a change in pay method as sufficient reason for the employee action.

In an unreported case, *Millson v Associated Western Ltd* [1989] EAT, the employer wished to switch to cashless pay for its employees. The employer offered a one-off payment to its employees to consent to the change. The trade union balloted its membership on this issue. The vote was overwhelmingly in favour of ceasing cash payments.

Only one employee refused to accept cashless pay. The company offered her assistance in getting to and from the bank, but she refused and two months later was dismissed. The appeal tribunal held that this was a fair dismissal, taking into consideration the conduct of the employer and the level of consultation that had taken place between the interested parties prior to initiating the change. An employer cannot insist that an employee opens a bank account.

For cash payments, it is necessary to:

- determine how many notes and coins of each denomination will be needed to make up each pay packet
- add up the total for each denomination to determine the quantities needed for the payroll
- order the currency from the bank (unless the amounts are small)
- have adequate security for collecting the cash and making up the payslips
- deliver the pay packets to employees, either obtaining a receipt from each employee or having a witness present
- store pay packets for absent employees in a safe
- have proper procedures for giving a pay packet to someone else for an absent employee
- chase up unclaimed wage packets
- return wage packets which still remain unclaimed to the employer's funds, but making no adjustment to the payroll data. The employee has six years in which to claim his or her wages.

For payments made by cheque, it is necessary to:

- decide whether payment should be made by open cheque or crossed cheque. A crossed cheque endorsed "a/c payee" is the ideal and preferred, but open cheques cannot be avoided for employees with no bank accounts. Recipients should be aware that an open cheque is similar to cash, and cannot be readily replaced if lost
- ensure that the employee receives the cheque. It is not necessary to obtain a receipt as a cheque legally is a receipt

- have a system for lost or mislaid cheques. The usual procedure is to stop a cheque and to issue a replacement after four working days.

For payments made by credit transfer it is necessary to:

- set up a system under BACS with the employer's bank, who will provide full details of operating the system
- have the bank account details of all employees
- allow sufficient time for processing the data.

Using Payroll Bureaux

Payroll bureaux can process the payroll for an employer. There are many such bureaux commercially available.

The efficient use of a bureau is best achieved by discussion with the organisation although these points should be considered.

- The employer must provide information to the bureau. The employer should consider whether the additional cost of using a bureau justifies its charges.
- The employer may provide the information in paper form or input directly from a computer terminal.
- A timetable needs to be prepared to ensure that deadlines are met.
- The employer needs to ensure that the bureau system is sufficiently flexible to cope with all the vagaries of the payroll, including any special payments or advances made.
- The employer should be satisfied about the creditworthiness and reliability of the bureau, usually by speaking to its existing customers.
- It should be clearly established whether or not the bureau will produce all the reports for HMRC.

Retention and Disposal of Records

Retention

Generally payroll and personnel records must, like other records of an organisation, be kept for three years for a private company, and for six years for a public company. There are no legal minima for partnerships and sole traders.

VAT records must be kept for six years and PAYE records for three years following the end of the tax year. Some records about working time must be kept for two years and National Minimum Wage records should be kept for three years after the end of the relevant pay reference period. Risk assessment records should be kept for a minimum of five years from the date on which they were first made. Medical and health surveillance records (generated in compliance with health and safety legislation) should be kept for at least 40 years.

However, it can be advisable to keep records for longer because:
- claims for tax can go back six years — 20 years if fraud is alleged
- if a company goes public, it can be required to produce records for the previous 10 years
- claims for defective goods may be made for 10 years
- claims for personal liability may be made within 12 years
- criminal prosecutions may be brought without time limit.

Archives

Old accounting and personnel records should be archived. The following points must be noted about archiving.
- The records need not be as accessible as current records, but must still be retrievable.
- Either adequate storage must be provided for existing records or arrangements must be made to keep them on microfilm or on a similar medium.
- If records are archived on a system such as on microfilm or optical disc, there must be adequate means for accessing and printing the record.
- Archives must be treated as being as confidential as current records.

Disposal of Records

When the period of retention has expired and there is no other reason to keep them, the records may be disposed of. The records should be securely destroyed, rather than just dumped.

CHAPTER 10

Government Schemes

Help for Unemployed

Types of Help

The following help is available to assist the unemployed to find work*:
- payment of Universal Credit (UC), Jobseeker's Allowance (JSA) or Employment and Support Allowance (ESA) if ill or disabled
- use of a Jobcentre Plus to find available work
- use of Jobcentre Plus Client Advisor to help the unemployed in finding work
- the Apprenticeship Scheme
- various special schemes to support the unemployed into employment or self-employment.

Note: *Similar but different schemes operate in Scotland and Wales.

The Work Programme

The Work Programme is delivered for Jobcentre Plus by external providers. It gives support to find and stay in work, and may last for up to two years. If the individual is receiving a JSA, he or she must take part in the Work Programme after nine months of unemployment if aged 18–24, or after 12 months if 25 or over, but may be able to join earlier. If receiving ESA and in the work-related activity group, the individual may have to join three months before the date the doctor expects him or her to be able to return to work. Similar rules will apply to recipients of UC. Exceptions may be made for carers and lone parents with children under five years old. Individuals who receive the support component of ESA, or who receive pension credit, may volunteer to join the Work Programme.

Work Clubs

Work clubs are run by local groups and provide advice and support to the unemployed. Taking part is voluntary.

Enterprise Clubs

Enterprise clubs are run by local groups and provide advice and support to the unemployed who are considering setting up in business. Taking part is voluntary.

New Enterprise Allowance

This is available to those who have been receiving JSA for at least six months and who are assessed as having a good business idea. It comprises a tax-free weekly allowance paid for up to 26 weeks and a loan of up to £1000. It is not available to those taking part in the Work Programme.

Work Experience

Individuals aged between 16 and 24 who have been receiving JSA for 13 weeks but are not yet required to join the Work Programme may volunteer for work experience. A placement will last between two and eight weeks. Under the Youth Contract, work experience will be offered to all 18- to 24-year-olds before they join the Work Programme.

Youth Contract

The Youth Contract will assist 18- to 24-year-olds into work by providing job subsidies for employers to take on individuals from the Work Programme and incentive payments for those offering apprenticeships.

Work Together

Individuals who are looking for work may carry out voluntary work while unemployed to improve their skills. The scheme is voluntary, but may not be undertaken by anyone required to join the Work Programme.

Sector-based Work Academies

Individuals who are aged 18 or over, and are receiving JSA, or ESA and in the work-related activity group, may be able to receive relevant training for up to six weeks.

Work Trials and Employment on Trial

A work trial allows an individual to try out a job and continue to receive benefits. The advantage to the employer is that there is no wage cost during the trial.

Employment on trial is a scheme under which an individual who has been in work for at least four but less than 12 weeks can leave the job without the reason for leaving affecting their benefit entitlement.

Work Schemes and Programmes for Disabled People

Access to Work and Work Choice are special schemes which assist disabled persons in taking up or continuing in employment.

Help to Move into Self-employment

The following help is available to move from unemployment to self-employment:
- business planning — helps the entrepreneur reduce financial risks
- business training — courses which cover all aspects of business
- the Department for Business, Energy & Industrial Strategy provides various forms of advice and guidance for small businesses
- local business links — free online resource and helpline
- bank loan guarantee schemes whereby the Government guarantees a bank loan which would otherwise not be available
- career development loans to help meet the cost of further training in order to improve job prospects.

Enterprise Finance Guarantee Scheme

The Enterprise Finance Guarantee scheme guarantees loans for small and medium-sized firms that have viable business proposals but have tried and failed to get a conventional loan. Under the scheme, a business which has a turnover of less than £41 million may claim a guarantee over 75% of a loan between £1000 and £1.2 million repayable over a period of three months to 10 years.

The Enterprise Finance Guarantee scheme was introduced because of the current economic climate and was set to run until 31 March 2011. It was then extended until 2014/15. It is still operating with several of the main banks offering the scheme.

Further information can be found on the British Business Bank website at *https://british-business-bank.co.uk*.

Education and Training

Basic Education

Main points:

- all children must receive full-time education from the ages of 5 to 16. From September 2013 children must either be in full-time education, an apprenticeship or full-time employment (over 20 hours per week) with part-time education until the end of the academic year in which they become 18
- the education may be from a state school, a private school or a private tutor
- the education must comply with the standards of the National Curriculum
- the national school examinations are the GCSE (introduced in 1986), usually taken at 16, and GCE AS-levels and A-levels, usually taken at 18
- a certificate of prevocational education has been available since 1986
- since 1991 all schools have kept a record of individual pupils' achievements
- further education is available from universities and colleges from the age of 16; many colleges became universities in 1993
- most universities offer a bachelor's degree as a first degree; the master's degree is a higher degree, except at Oxford and Cambridge and in Scotland; above that, doctorates are awarded for post-graduate research.

From September 2008, 14- to 19-year-olds may study for the diploma, a more practical qualification offering hands-on experience as well as classroom learning. The diploma can be combined with GCSEs and A-levels.

Professional Qualifications

In addition to school examinations and university degrees, there are many professional bodies which offer qualifications, often indicated by designatory letters. In some areas, such as accountancy, law and medicine, possession of such a qualification is a condition of being allowed to practise in that field.

Vocational Qualifications

National Vocational Qualifications (NVQs) and Scottish Vocational Qualifications (SVQs) are offered at five main levels.

- Level 1 — basic competence in a range of routine activities.
- Level 2 — competence in a broader and more demanding range of activities.
- Level 3 — competence in skilled areas in a wide range of activities including complex, non-routine activities and possibly supervision.
- Level 4 — competence in complex, technical or professional activities, including supervision.
- Level 5 — competence in the application of computer techniques in unpredictable contexts, significant responsibility for the work of others, allocation of resources and considerable personal accountability.

Training for People under 25

- Entry to Employment (E2E) — a chance to learn new skills to at least NVQ level 2, for under 18s.
- Intermediate and Advanced Level Apprenticeships (England and Wales) — to learn high-level skills and qualifications to NVQ level 3, Higher Apprenticeships to NVQ level 4–7.
- Time off for study or training — a way of getting qualifications and experience for under 18s while in a job, to at least NVQ level 2.

CHAPTER 11

Miscellaneous

Rehabilitation of Offenders

Generally, a person convicted of a minor offence does not have to disclose that conviction to a prospective employer after a rehabilitation period. Note that an employer is still free to employ an unrehabilitated offender; the law relates only to disclosure. The rehabilitation periods are as follows.

Rehabilitation Periods from 10 March 2014 (Custodial Sentences)

Sentence length	Current rehabilitation period (applies from date of conviction)	New rehabilitation period is period of sentence plus the "buffer" period below which applies from end of sentence)
0–6 months	7 years	2 years
6–30 months	10 years	4 years
30 months–4 years	Never spent	7 years
Over 4 years	Never spent	Never spent

Rehabilitation Periods from 10 March 2014 (Non-custodial Sentences)

Sentence	Current rehabilitation period (applies from date of conviction)	Buffer period (will apply from end of sentence)
Community order (& Youth Rehabilitation Order)	5 years	1 year
Fine	5 years	1 year (from date of conviction)
Absolute discharge	6 months	None
Conditional discharge, referral order, reparation order, action plan order, supervision order, bind over order, hospital order	Various — mostly between one year and length of the Order	Period of order

Rehabilitation Periods Prior to 10 March 2014

Sentence	Rehabilitation period
Imprisonment for between 6 and 30 months	10 years*
Imprisonment for 6 months or less	7 years*
Fines, compensation, community service and certain other sentences; probation (if convicted on or after 3 February 1995)	5 years*
Absolute discharge	6 months
Probation (those convicted before 3 February 1995), binding over, conditional discharge, supervision order, care order	1 year or until the order expires (whichever is longer)
Detention for between 6 and 30 months (certain sentences imposed on young offenders)	5 years

Sentence	Rehabilitation period
Detention for 6 months or less (certain sentences imposed on young offenders)	3 ½ years
Detention centre order	3 years
Security training (abolished in 2000) and attendance centre orders	1 year from expiry of order
Hospital order under the Mental Health Acts	later of 5 years from conviction and 2 years from expiry of the order

*This period is halved if the person was under 18 when the sentence was imposed.

Note: Imprisonment for more than 30 months is never regarded as "spent". For the following occupations, even minor offences never become "spent":

- solicitors, barristers, judges, coroners and other lawyers
- accountants
- medical staff
- those employed by courts or the probation service
- police officers
- teachers
- operators of the national lottery
- those employed in social services
- those in jobs which involve working with people under the age of 18.

Jury Service

On 6 April 2004, the **Employment Relations Act 2004** came into effect providing employees who are summoned for jury service, or have had time off for jury service, with greater protection.

The regulations provide that employees have the right not to be subjected to any detriment for being summoned for jury service or having time off for jury service.

There is no right to be paid by an employer while absent on jury service. A detriment, therefore, excludes not paying employees' their normal remuneration for the period that they are on jury service, unless the contract of employment specifies otherwise. If an employer chooses not to pay, jurors may claim compensation for loss of earnings. The current loss of earnings allowances are as follows.

Jury Service — Loss of Earnings Allowances

Time spent on jury service		Loss of earnings allowance
Up to and including 4 hours	In the first 10 days of jury service	£32.47
	On day 11 up to the 200th day of jury service	£64.95
	On the 201st and all subsequent days	£114.03
More than four hours	In the first 10 days of jury service	£64.95
	On day 11 up to the 200th day of jury service	£129.91
	On the 201st and all subsequent days	£228.06

Jurors may also claim a subsistence allowance for their time away. The current rates are as follows.

Jury Service — Subsistence Allowances

Period of absence	Maximum daily allowance
Up to and including 10 hours	£5.71
10 hours or more	£12.17
Overnight stay	Accommodation will be arranged by the Court

Travel allowance may also be claimed by jurors at the current rates shown below.

Jury Service — Travel Allowances

Mode of Transport	Allowance
Train, underground or bus	The cost of the ticket (2nd class return fare)

Mode of Transport	Allowance
Motorcycle	31.4p per mile
Motorcycle if no alternative public transport available	29.8 per mile
Bicycle	9.6p per mile
Car	31.4p per mile
Car if no alternative public transport available	42.5 p per mile
Car supplement if other jurors are passengers	For the first passenger, 4.2p per mile. For each additional passenger, 3.2p per mile

Parking fees will be paid only where permission to claim for them has been given before travel and taxi fares will be paid only where permission to use a taxi has been given.

Employees also have the right not to be unfairly dismissed for being absent from work on jury service. However, where an employer can show that its circumstances are such that the employee's absence would cause substantial injury to its business and communicates this to the employee, and where the employee unreasonably fails or refuses to apply for excusal or deferral, this subsection does not apply.

Notice Periods

An employee generally has the right to a period of notice, as set out in the contract of employment. This must not be less than the statutory minimum.

Minimum Periods of Statutory Notice

Length of continuous service	Period of notice
less than one month	none
1 month to 2 years	one week
2 to 12 years	one week per year of service
12 or more years	12 weeks

The notice period may be dispensed with and no compensation offered in lieu if the employee commits an offence so serious that it is incompatible with continuing employment. This is known as "summary dismissal".

If an employer dismisses an employee without notice, other than as a summary dismissal, the employer is obliged to pay the employee for the notice period. If this is allowed for in accordance with the contract of employment, the payment is subject to tax and National Insurance. If not, it will usually be regarded as compensation and be free of tax and National Insurance.

Death of an Employee

The employment consequences of the death of an employee are:
- the employment is ended with payment due to date of death
- it is courteous to express sympathy to the employee's family
- any SMP is paid to the end of the week of death; SSP to the day of death
- outstanding payments must be made to the employee's personal representative
- HMRC is advised by sending all three parts of the P45 marked "D"
- no National Insurance is payable in the pay period of death
- the HSE must be informed without delay if an employee dies as a result of a work-related injury, or dies within 12 months of sustaining any such injury (as per the **Reporting of Injuries, Diseases and Dangerous Occurrences Regulations 1995**)
- a spouse's pension, life insurance claim or pension guarantee may become payable
- the personnel records need amending
- if death occurred at work, notification to the HSE and the police must be made
- if the employee was under notice for what is held to be unfair dismissal, the date of death is substituted for the date of dismissal
- any proceedings outstanding between employer and employee only continue if the personal representative so directs
- any tax rebates withheld for being on strike are paid.

Insurance Requirements for Employers

An employer must:

- have at least £5 million in insurance cover for personal injury or disease sustained by employees during their employment
- display the insurance certificate on the premises. Employers must ensure they display the certificate where employees can see it ie on the company intranet.

Personnel Disclosure in Accounting Records

Employees

The following information on personnel must be disclosed in the annual accounts of a limited company.

- Total employee costs.
- Social security costs of employees (ie employer's National Insurance).
- Pension costs of employees.
- Average number of employees.
- Average number of employees by category.
- Statement of policy on disabled employees (if the organisation has 250 or more employees).

Directors

The following information must be disclosed about directors.

- The names of all who were directors during the financial year.
- The total emoluments paid to directors.
- The chairman's emoluments.
- The emoluments of the highest paid director.
- The number of directors who received emoluments (in each band of £5000) above £60,000.
- The number of directors who have waived emoluments, and the amount waived.
- The aggregate amount of current and past directors' pensions.
- The aggregate amount paid to directors for loss of office.
- Sums paid to third parties for directors' services.
- Details of contracts in which the directors have an interest, and details of that interest.

Fines

Certain criminal penalties attract fines quoted as being at levels 1 to 5. From 1 October 1992, these levels have been:

Fine Levels

Level	Fine
1	£200
2	£500
3	£1000
4	£2500
5	£5000

CHAPTER 12

Commonly-used Abbreviations

Acas	Advisory Conciliation and Arbitration Service
AEI	Average Earnings Index
AEO	attachment of earnings order
AML	additional maternity leave
AVC	additional voluntary contribution (to pension scheme)
AWE	Average Weekly Earnings
BACS	Bankers Automated Clearing Service
BEIS	Department for Business, Energy & Industrial Strategy
BST	British Summer Time
CAB	Citizens' Advice Bureau
CAC	Central Arbitration Committee
CBI	Confederation of British Industry
ccc	cwmni cyfyngedig cyhoeddus (Welsh for "public limited company")
CGT	capital gains tax
CHAPS	Clearing House Automatic Payment System
CIPD	Chartered Institute of Personnel and Development
CJEU	Court of Justice of the European Union
co	company

c-o	contracted-out (of SERPS)
COMP	contracted-out money purchase scheme (pensions)
COSR	contracted-out salary related scheme (pensions)
CPI	Consumer Prices Index
CRB	Criminal Records Bureau — an executive agency of the Home Office
CSA	Child Support Agency
CV	curriculum vitae
cyf	cyfyngedig (Welsh for "limited")
DB	defined benefit (pension scheme)
DBS	Disclosure and Barring Service
DC	defined contribution (pension scheme)
DEO	deduction of earnings order
DH	Department of Health
DLA	disability living allowance
dob	date of birth
DPA	Data Protection Act 1998
DSE	display screen equipment
DWP	Department for Work and Pensions
EAT	Employment Appeal Tribunal
EEA	European Economic Area
EC	European Community
ECHR	European Court of Human Rights
ECB	European Central Bank
ECJ	European Court of Justice
EDT	effective date of termination
EEA	European Economic Area
EHRC	Equality and Human Rights Commission
ERA	Employment Rights Act 1996

ESA	Employment and Support Allowance
ETO	economic, technical or organisational reason for dismissal (TUPE)
EU	European Union
EWC	expected week of childbirth (SMP)/ European Works Council
FSA	Financial Services Authority
GAYE	give as you earn
GB	Great Britain
GDPR	General Data Protection Regulation
GMT	Greenwich Mean Time
GOQ	genuine occupational qualifications (discrimination law)
GOR	genuine occupational requirements (discrimination law)
GPP	group personal pension
HMRC	Her Majesty's Revenue & Customs
HRM	human resources management
HSE	Health and Safety Executive
HSWA	Health and Safety at Work, etc Act 1974
ICO	Information Commissioner's Office
ICTA	Income and Corporation Taxes Act 1988
ISA	Independent Safeguarding Authority
ITEPA	Income Tax (Earnings and Pensions) Act 2003
JSA	Jobseeker's Allowance
LEL	lower earnings limit
MA	Maternity Allowance
MPP	maternity pay period
NCVQ	National Council for Vocational Qualifications
NEST	National Employment Savings Trust

NI	National Insurance
NIC	National Insurance contributions
NMW	National Minimum Wage
NVQ	National Vocational Qualification
OML	ordinary maternity leave
pa	per annum
PAYE	pay as you earn
PCP	provision, criterion or practice
PHI	permanent health insurance
PIW	period of incapacity for work (SSP)
POCA	Protection of Children Act
PoVA	Protection of Vulnerable Adults
PPF	Pension Protection Fund
PRP	profit-related pay
PSA	PAYE settlement agreement
QCA	Qualifications and Curriculum Authority
QW	qualifying week
RIPA	Regulation of Investigatory Powers Act 2000
RPI	Retail Prices Index
RSI	repetitive strain injury
S2P	State Second Pension
SAP	statutory adoption pay
SER	small employers' relief
SERPS	State Earnings Related Pension Scheme
SHP	Stakeholder Pension Scheme
ShPP	Statutory Shared Parental Pay
SI	statutory instrument
SMP	statutory maternity pay

SOSR	some other substantial reason
SPL	Shared Parental Leave
SPP	statutory paternity pay
SRP	statutory redundancy pay
SSP	statutory sick pay
SVQ	Scottish Vocational Qualification
TICER	Transnational Information and Consultation of Employees Regulations 1999
TPI	Tax and Prices Index
TSO	The Stationery Office
TUC	Trades Union Congress
TULR(C)A	Trade Union and Labour Relations (Consolidation) Act 1992
TUPE	Transfer of Undertakings (Protection of Employment) Regulations 2006
TURERA	Trade Union Reform and Employment Rights Act 1993
UC	Universal Credit
UEL	upper earnings limit
UK	United Kingdom
UKBA	UK Border Agency — a shadow agency of the Home Office
VAT	value added tax
VBS	vetting and barring scheme
VDU	visual display unit
WTR	Working Time Regulations 1998

CHAPTER 13

Directory of Useful Addresses

Advisory Conciliation and
Arbitration Service (Acas)
Euston Tower
286 Euston Road
London NW1 3JJ
Helpline: 0300 123 1100
Website: *www.acas.org.uk*

Business Disability Forum
Nutmeg House
60 Gainsford Street
London SE1 2NY
Tel: 020 7403 3020
Website: *www.
businessdisabilityforum.org.uk*

CBI
Cannon Place
78 Cannon Street
London EC4N 6HN
Tel: 020 7379 7400
Website: *www.cbi.org.uk*

Central Arbitration Committee
Fleetbank House
2-6 Salisbury Square
London EC4Y 8JX
Tel: 0330 109 3610
Website: *www.gov.uk/government/
organisations/central-arbitration-
committee*

Certification Officer
Certification Office
Lower Ground Floor
Fleetbank House
2-6 Salisbury Square
London EC4Y 8JX
Tel: 0330 109 3610
Website: *www.gov.uk/government/
organisations/certification-officer*

Chartered Institute of Personnel
and Development (CIPD)
151 The Broadway
London SW19 1JQ
Tel: 020 8612 6200
Website: *www.cipd.co.uk*

Companies House
Crown Way
Cardiff CF14 3UZ
Tel: 0303 1234 500
Website: *www.gov.uk/government/
organisations/companies-house*

Department for Business, Energy
& Industrial Strategy
1 Victoria Street
London SW1H 0ET
Tel: 020 7215 5000
Website: *www.gov.uk/government/
organisations/department-for-business-
energy-and-industrial-strategy*

Department for Education
Piccadilly Gate
Store Street
Manchester M1 2WD
Tel: 0370 000 2288
Website: *www.gov.uk/government/
organisations/department-for-
education*

Department for Work and Pensions
Caxton House
Tothill Street
London SW1H 9NA
Tel: 020 7340 4395
Website: *www.gov.uk/government/
organisations/department-for-work-
pensions*

Disclosure and Barring Service
(DBS)
DBS Customer Services
PO Box 3961
Royal Wootton Bassett SN4 4HF
Tel: 03000 200 190
Website: *www.gov.uk/government/
organisations/disclosure-and-barring-
service*

Employment Appeal Tribunal
(EAT) *(England and Wales)*
Second Floor
Fleetbank House
2–6 Salisbury Square
London EC4Y 8AE
Tel: 020 7273 1041
Website: *www.gov.uk/courts-
tribunals/employment-appeal-tribunal*

Employment Appeal Tribunal
(EAT) *(Scotland)*
52 Melville Street
Edinburgh EH3 7HF
Tel: 0131 225 3963
Website: *www.gov.uk/courts-
tribunals/employment-appeal-tribunal*

Employment Tribunals Service
(England and Wales)
Contact Centre
PO Box 10218
Leicester LE1 8EG
Tel: 0300 123 1024
Website: *www.gov.uk/courts-
tribunals/employment-tribunal*

Employment Tribunals Service
(Scotland)
Contact Centre
PO Box 27105
Glasgow G2 9JR
Website: *www.gov.uk/courts-tribunals/employment-tribunal*

Equality Advisory and Support
Service
Helpline: 0808 800 0082
Website: *www.equalityadvisoryservice.com*

Equality Commission for Northern
Ireland
Equality House
7–9 Shaftesbury Square
Belfast BT2 7DP
Tel: 028 90 500 600
Website: *www.equalityni.org*

European Commission
(Representation in the UK)
Europe House
32 Smith Square
London SW1P 3EU
Tel: 020 7973 1992
Website: *www.ec.europa.eu/unitedkingdom*

European Parliament Information
Office
Europe House
32 Smith Square
London SW1P 3EU
Tel: 020 7227 4300
Website: *www.europarl.europa.eu/unitedkingdom*

Health and Safety Executive
Redgrave Court
Merton Road
Bootle
Merseyside L20 7HS
Tel: 0151 951 4000
Incident Contact Centre: 0345 300 9923
Online report form: *www.hse.gov.uk/riddor*
Website: *www.hse.gov.uk*

HM Revenue & Customs
National Insurance Contributions
and Employers Office
BX9 1BX
Helpline: 0300 200 3200
Website: *www.gov.uk/government/organisations/hm-revenue-customs*

Home Office
Direct Communications Unit
2 Marsham Street
London SW1P 4DF
Tel: 020 7035 4848
Website: *www.gov.uk/government/organisations/home-office*

Home Office UK Visas and
Immigration
Employers' helpline: 0300 123 4699
Website: *www.gov.uk/government/organisations/uk-visas-and-immigration*

HSE Books
TSO Customer Services
PO Box 29
Norwich NR3 1GN
Tel: 0333 202 5070
Website: *http://books.hse.gov.uk*

Information Commissioner
Wycliffe House
Water Lane
Wilmslow
Cheshire SK9 5AF
Tel: 0303 123 1113
Website: *https://ico.org.uk*

Ministry of Justice
102 Petty France
London SW1H 9AJ
Tel: 01633 630 942
Website: *www.gov.uk/government/
organisations/ministry-of-justice*

Office of Manpower Economics
8th Floor
Fleetbank House
2-6 Salisbury Square
London EC4Y 8JX
Tel: 020 7211 8165
Website: *www.gov.uk/government/
organisations/office-of-manpower-
economics*

Office for National Statistics
Customer Contact Centre
Room D265
Government Buildings
Cardiff Road
Newport
South Wales NP10 8XG
Tel: 0845 601 3034
Website: *www.ons.gov.uk*

Pensions Advisory Service
11 Belgrave Road
London SW1V 1RB
Tel: 0800 011 3797
Website: *www.
pensionsadvisoryservice.org.uk*

Pensions Ombudsman
10 South Colonnade
Canary Wharf E14 4PU
Tel: 0800 917 4487
Website: *www.pensions-ombudsman.
org.uk*

Scottish Government
St Andrew's House
Regent Road
Edinburgh EH1 3DG
Tel: 0300 244 4000
Website: *www.gov.scot*

TSO (The Stationery Office)
St Crispins
Duke Street
Norwich NR3 1PD
Tel: 0333 202 5070
Website: *www.tsonline.co.uk*

Trades Union Congress
Congress House
23–28 Great Russell Street
London WC1B 3LS
Tel: 020 7636 4030
Website: *www.tuc.org.uk*

UK Intellectual Property Office
Concept House
Cardiff Road
Newport
South Wales NP10 8QQ
Tel: 0300 300 2000
Website: *www.gov.uk/government/ organisations/intellectual-property-office*

Welsh Assembly Government
Cathays Park
Cardiff CF10 3NQ
Tel: 0300 060 4400
Website: *http://gov.wales*

INDEX

Y

Z